Diary of the ~~~~~~

From
Dust to Dust

Australia's Cricket Tour
of India - 2013

Dave Cornford and

Jeremy Pooley

CONTENTS

ACKNOWLEDGMENTS

To the 17 members of the Australian Cricket Team, the Coach and all 120 members of Team Management, without whose unwitting cooperation this diary could not have been written.

A special tribute to the 17th Man's growing brigade of fans. If we can add some small pleasure to your day - however you choose to waste it - drawing on broad lessons from the great game of cricket, we shall have achieved more than we thought possible.

And to the 17th Man, who persuaded us over a few drinks that his peculiar back room insights should be shared, and our families and friends who have read his daily musings out of obligation and sympathy for idle minds. You do not know what fires you have lit.

1 PRELIMINARIES

FEBRUARY 14

I received the call up from Cricket Australia this morning. It would have been better if I'd been named as an official member of the squad, but under the circumstances, being the extra secret batsmen on tour to cover for the Captain's dodgy back is better than hanging around in Oz. There will be no action at finals time after our appalling Shield season, and I'm sick of my mates paying me out after I was passed in at the IPL Auction last week. US$100,000 sounds like a lot, but Warnie always said it costs more to live there than you realize, even though mobile phone plans are fairly cheap.

Most of the team has already left for the tour. It was certainly a second string team that didn't quite make the runs against the Windies last night.

From what I can tell, the team has split up into little "in-groups" and headed off for "specialist training":

- The fast bowlers are in Chennai, acclimatizing to the heat. I bet this means they're practicing minimizing the effects of shrinkage in the ice bath.

- The top order is in transit after a debacle in QLD. Team Management had organized a dust bowl for them to practice on, but being 35 km from Rockhampton, the whole thing's gone pear shaped in a pool of mud. They can't even salvage some PR from this debacle by helping flood victims because the whole thing is a massive secret.

- Wicky's kit was lost in transit and ended up in Phuket. He's gone chasing it, against Team Management's advice. There is one essential part of his luggage that he needed to keep eye on, apparently…he had better make it in time for the tour match on Saturday or one of the batsmen will be making an idiot of themselves behind the stumps.

- The spinners are in Mumbai at an acting school practicing not giving anything away to the batsmen, after one of the wristy batsmen dispatched another one of their spot pies to the mid-wicket boundary. Would they learn more about spin in Tony Abbott's press office?

I guess someone has a plan for all this to work so that we win a test or two on this tour. Recent tour history does not bear repeating.

A suspicious package arrived while I was on the phone. The housekeeper signed for it, even though it was marked Strictly Private & Confidential. It contained a large sample jar of a special "Surviving the Subcontinent" supplement from some sports medicine guy I hadn't heard of before. How he knew to send it to me, I'll never know. I grabbed a face mask and gloves as soon as I realized what it was, parceled it up, wrote return to sender on it, and put it in the postbox at the shops. I don't want any traces of that nasty stuff on my person if I am tested at the medical this afternoon.

The medical was uneventful, although the bitter quack who has been omitted from the tour party was not gentle at any stage of the examination - talk about ball tampering......

No drug test today, just a 25 page legal document I was instructed to sign under which I guaranteed that I would only eat scotch finger biscuits and drink apple cider outside of regular meals on tour.

A packing list has just come in on the email. I need to get to the airport for the late flight out tonight.

Wish me luck!

FEBRUARY 15

I think it's OK to use the iPad now. We've made it through Singapore – next stop Chennai. I don't think the main touring party enjoyed the luxury of Premium Economy, but it could have been worse. The ABC correspondent, who the BCCI has snubbed by not accrediting for the tour, is stuck up the back near the dunny door in the "lots of kids screaming" section.

After the shock of it all, Anthea (my partner) was delighted with my call up. As she said, a bit unexpected given my recent run of form, but I didn't get selected when I was actually scoring runs, so, like umpiring decisions, you just have to take it as it comes.

I saw Mum and Dad before I left. They loaded the two of us with snags, baked potatoes, 4 veg and a slab of cheesecake. My favourite fare, although a little heavy just before a flight. Dad was a bit strange, I mean stranger than normal at family gatherings, and absented himself during dessert, claiming he had 'indigestion', to take the spaniel for a leak round the block. He had a grim look. I know how he felt – 17th bloody man, and he has to keep it under his hat for a while. Not quite the triumphant payback for 15 years of backyard arm-rolling, 1,000 hours of sunburn and schoolboy cricket, not to mention scoring (badly), coaching U9s – U12s with all those feral parents, and controversial stints as an umpire. I get that. How does he think I feel?

Mum was pleased. "17th man," she said. "You never know in India," she said (she has never been there). "You can only eat vindaloo and Gungadins Balls for so long before 4 or 5 of them keel over and you're out there taking guard in a Test, sweating like a thoroughbred. You'll play."

I don't know about that, but at least I'm on the plane. There is one Shield player in particular who missed selection that will be dark when he finds out I've scored a ticket – but that will teach him. That huge spat in the dressing room cancelled out his 4 Shield tons this season. I wish I could send him a friendly text to gloat.

The food is coming around again. I guess I'll follow Nanna's Travel Tips and have the curry. She reckons eating curry on Air India should be safe. There is one thing you can bank on about any "western" food option – it's been back and forth between Chennai and Singapore so many times it could have earned an upgrade to business class on points. Lucky salad, I say.

I had better get some sleep as well. I'll have to stay awake through the tour game tomorrow. It's sure to be a yawn sitting around twiddling my thumbs watching the team fumble around in the dust. I don't need to embarrass myself this early in the tour, so I've sketched brief profiles of the sixteen players selected before me, along with the support crew.

The Players:

Mr. Bean (Opener): Debonair. As casual as you like. Precise kit packer. Prankster. Jazz player. IT man. Thinker.

Puff (Opener): Short and powerfully built backwoodsman. A big six man. Loves a chirp. Quick. Dives for everything. Hands bigger than Wicky's gloves. Tweeter.

Lucky (No3): Lefty. Unstoppable when in form. Straight shooter. Desperate to prove a point in India.

Hollywood (No4): Tall, well-built surfer class all-rounder batsman. Takes time alone to reflect, relax, renew. Joker and gentleman. A true cricket brain when in song.

The Captain (No5): The consummate cricket professional. Leads from the front "power of one", Type-A. Loves winning Tests. Footwork like a ballet dancer. Tweeter.

Wicky (Wicketkeeper): Short and hairy. Communal spitter due to larynx injury removing a stump in U13 20/20 final. Hapless butt of jokes. Keeper of the team song with Plopper. Learning to tweet.

Jacka (All rounder): Bob the Builder type. Jack of all trades, recognised master of none. In India to prove a point. Humorist and one-time stand-up comic. Tweeter.

The Freak (Quick): Reliable 'Go To' man when behind the eight ball. Takes the mickey. Innovator. Drawer, pastel painter. Easily bored

Rocket Man (Quick): Young clean tear-away with occasional reverse swing. Huge wraps. Heavy mortgage on his future. Guitar player, dancer and Boy band lover. Tweeter.

Mr. Darcy (Quick): Engaging dark hair dark-eyed striker with an action smooth as silk. The right word for every occasion. Ladies' man. Tweeter.

Plopper (No1 Spinner): Test regular. Only ever wanted to bowl for Australia. Slept with a ball since he was six. Will play even if not selected.

Trapper (Reserve): Spare whatever. Likes running out with the physio when players are injured and at drinks with messages for the players. An optimist.

The Reject Club

Gipper (Spinner): Test discard. Spins the ball in a left-right breeze, sometimes. Occult expert.

Rabbit (Spinner): Young. Short like a rabbit. Nice guy. Third option spinner if no one else is available. Working hard on his batting.

Mantis (Quick): Tall beanpole. Second change swinger. Fitness fanatic. Yoga man and ocean swimmer.

Prof (Batsman, occasional keeper): The curly-haired bespectacled brains of the team. Triple math major. Soothsayer, and satirist. Loathes curry but loves India. Thinks only birds tweet.

Support Crew

Coach: Brown-eyed giant. Former insolvency practitioner (somewhere south of the Cape). Styled himself as a performance turnaround expert after sharing a bottle of bubbly with the late Bob Woolmer in Kingston, Jamaica in 2007. Rates the current Australian Tour of India as his biggest career challenge. Shows mild bi-polar symptoms. Risk-taker under pressure. Likes a bet

Darren (team psychologist): Catholic seminarian turned clinical psychologist (Oxford) after a stint as first XV rugby coach with a name public school. Member, IOC Banned Substances Committee 2010-2011. Chummy with the Chairman of Selectors who signed him up on a "losing tour" so he can finish his PhD in predictive on-field decision-making. Greeny. Occult expert and exorcist.

Team management: A motley crew of 15 Gen Y seasonal fruit-pickers from the Lachlan Valley, NSW, hired on the cheap by CA to manage press (keep them away), book team events, accommodation, and repair player kit etc. (Money saved has been added to the player bonus pool). Otherwise they are a waste of space.

Massai (team masseur): Warrior. Sought a city change in 2007 as back-walker in the Dallas Cowboy's defensive unit. Minor scandal with the Cowgirl's masseuse. Transferred to the Mathilda's in 2008, and to the men's Test squad after the Ashes defeat in 2012. Arthritic knuckles. Champion muscle tenderiser. Darren likes him. He thinks Darren is a prat.

FEBRUARY 16
Day 1 – Tour Match - Chennai

I have never been on an overseas tour before. The chaos on the first morning was something to behold. This is a relatively inexperienced team, so the simple things like getting up on time for breakfast having already packed your kit were beyond some of the bowlers.

Even though it's only a short trip from the hotel to the ground, the jockeying for prime seats on the bus, everyone staking their claim for the rest of the tour, had to be seen to be believed. If the spinners bowl with the guile that was on display as they shimmied into front row seats, they might get some wickets.

The toss went against us and the team was sent out into the field, which might have been a good thing to get straight into it – 30 degrees and not so humid, with only a chance of rain.

The talk at lunch was dominated not by the lack of

wickets taken in the session but by the news from South Africa that the Blade Runner was behind bars, accused of murdering his girlfriend. No-one had actually met him before, so all the talk of hot tempers and gun toting was in no way based in fact or firsthand experience.

Lunch itself was a lavish feast as usual at these smaller grounds, with the locals trying very hard to impress. After half an hour, not even the notoriously ravenous non-playing squad members had put a dent in the spread.

Things should have settled down in the afternoon session, but it was not to be. It was a bit weird in the dressing room, as the membership of The Reject Club – the 5 members of the team not named in the 12 – was not the usual "fish that John West Rejects." The team on the field was stacked with "maybes", so instead of slacking off all day, we had the Captain hanging around like a bad smell keeping an eye on us. One of the batsmen tried to convince everyone, including himself, that he was being rested and was really a dead cert' for the first test. We kept winding him up by implying he was going to be a tour-long member of The Reject Club, offering him entry into our exclusive sweep and asking him what sized "I'm a Reject" t-shirt he wanted – but he was having none of it.

The day ended with a stack of runs on the board for India A. The spinners had a lot of practice acting pained at the injustice of an alleged jaffa being dispatched to the boundary. The Indian players, none of whom are down to play in the first test, were all keen to show the selectors what a grave injustice it was that they were left out of their squad for the real game next week. 4/338 – ouch.

FEBRUARY 17
Day 2 – Tour Match - Chennai

I spoke to Thea last night – she was at Mum and Dad's again. She was pleased I arrived safely. "Was the bed ok? Did you ask for an extra pillow? Have you had a beer with the Captain yet? I know you get on with him. He'll get you on the field." Poor Thea. After reading The Captain's comments in the Times of India (TOI) yesterday under the headline "Hardest Test Ever" it's pretty clear what he wants. It's not about what you say, he said, it is about what you do. "Perform well on the field. That's all we want".

Dad was in the background with the dog. I think he's still miffed that I wasn't selected for this game. "Three days is about your limit. At least they could have named you 12th man". I missed the rest. The dog was barking and to be frank it was hard to distinguish them.

I received a package by courier from home when I returned to the Hotel - six books about strength through adversity? I gave the one about Pistorius to the Team Manager. I wouldn't be caught out with it now. He cracked a sly grin saying he would take care of it, which may well mean using it page by page if he ever gets caught short later in the tour. I'll read the Steve Waugh book first and pick up on the 2001 India tour.

The spinners invited me to the bar after dinner. They needed something to settle their nerves. The three of them picked up 3/260 odd, figures hard to stomach if today is any harbinger of what is to come. Plopper mumbled over and over something about patience and consistency. I was ready to call for Darren, team psychologist (resident nutcase) when he broke a grin mouthing Elton's 'Rocket Man' instead. Anything to avert mental disintegration he said. The Captain nodded approvingly from the next table. "It's only the curtain raiser" he said "Forget today. Learn from it. Everything will turn."

And it did. The first 2 hours were gobbled up by rain. The Captain called a team meeting to unpack our perceptions of yesterday's performance. He began with two simple questions - What had we learned yesterday? What were we going to do differently to take the initiative? The bowlers isolated the odd practical insight – bowl faster, don't throw it up – from the witticisms and other radical suggestions this form of open consultation attracts.

Whatever they did, it was hard to see what, the spinners cleaned up the tail for about 100. Our lads set about clearing the slate wielding the bat to all parts of the field. The crack of willow on leather became so regular I put aside the Times of India to take in this rhythmic spectacle untroubled by the shimmering heat of the day. The Captain finally relaxed, removing his sprigs from the meat of my shoulder. I didn't mind. The double folded handkerchief stitched to the inside of my playing shirt worked a treat.

When the first wicket fell lbw to a spinner – read into this what you wish – the mood refocused sensing the next wicket stand might rightly be one of the vital moments in the game. Number 3 and 4 fell in quick succession again to spinners to leave us shaky at stumps at 4/131. Maybe we can hold out to avoid the follow on. Another learning day – double ouch!

FEBRUARY 18
Day 3 – Tour Match - Chennai

We were pleased to get out of today with some dignity intact. Well, all of us apart from Plopper who ended up locked outside the dressing room in the wan light of the late afternoon wearing nothing but a jock strap and a wry smile. We would have had an excuse for not hearing his endless bashing on the door if it had been the last day of a series win and Khe Sanh was blaring out. Instead, we sat there in an eerie silence, listening to him bash and panic for well over ten minutes - it reminded us of his batting.

A more solid performance in the second dig saw the game meander along to a draw in the end. The fielding was a little unusual at times – deep third man had a touch of mange in the hour before tea. A couple of the lads batted well overall, and must be feeling a touch more confident. For the most part though, I doubt that the Indian test spinners will be doing anything other than licking their lips tonight.

News from Mumbai that the Southern Stars had added the World Cup to their bulging trophy cabinet the previous evening by walloping the West Indies was no help. They played well, but when it comes down to it, it's all about whether our top six can come to terms with the Indian spinners. After our scratchy display against their second stringers, things aren't looking good with the first test starting in a few days.

A special "spin clinic" has been called by the coach for tomorrow for everyone in the touring party. It will be interesting to see where that happens – every set of practice nets we have been offered by the hosts is as green as Kermit the Frog, while the pitch for the first test is sure to be a dust bowl.

FEBRUARY 19

The Coach came round banging on doors early. Very Rude. Wicky was asleep, his gloved hand all but suffocating him. I tied his ankles to the bedpost, yelled fire and slammed the door. If I'd thought to film it, I would be a shoe-in for winning Funniest Home Videos.

The newspaper boy jammed a copy of the latest TOI under my arm as I turned to board the bus, flicking a perfect "how's your father" at Wicky who was trapped in the revolving door. Not his day already. The headline told it all: 'Aussie Bats No Match for Our Spinners,' book ended by the equally subtle back page: 'Aussie batsman humbled. India on Top.' I might get a game after all.

We got to the ground at 6.30 am. It was padlocked. Coach threatened to drive the bus through the gate before the grounds man reluctantly agreed to let us in. We set up a searchlight on a couple of rickety stools to light up the practice wicket and a couple of the lads rolled it a few times. Coach produced a can of spray paint to mark out the crease.

He waved us in real close. Pointing to the crease he said "Either full stretch forward or step back. Don't get trapped on the crease! That's it! That's it! Have you got that? We stay here today, maybe all day, until you get it right."

The first two in were about to question the rather murky morning light, but realized that it was not the time or place to be precious about such niceties as the batting conditions.

The spinners bowled all morning, brilliantly, and a change-up compared to Day 1 of the practice game. No one could hit a thing. Coach kept yelling "Forward!" or "BACK! BACK!" over and over again. It didn't seem to make much difference.

We broke for lunch sporting a ravenous hunger, only to find an untidy spread of vegemite sandwiches provided by our Hotel. No one touched the fruit.

The Prof. found a hose to wash down the bowlers

when they least expected it. Mid delivery stride was about right – it was stinking hot. The Coach yelled at us all afternoon. "Watch it from the hand. Be mindful. Bat with purpose. Get it in the middle." Late in the day some of us started to do just that. It felt good. The Captain called it quits at 4.30pm.

We found the Coach in the sheds, sweating like a bullock, cutting the TOI into little squares, page by page, with a dirty pair of fingernail scissors from the medical kit. A battered Ouija board lay at his feet. Darren escorted him to the bus muttering soothing thoughts into his deaf left ear. Then Wicky led us in the team song, taking a break during the second verse to cough up a fly and praise the Lord for recovering his kit and its mysterious cargo from a disused subway station in Moscow.

The Captain invited us to the Hotel Bar on our return, Coach's shout. The first frothy barely touched the sides. Coach shouted a second before the boys relaxed.

Tomorrow the Captain announces the team for the first test. I looked for Coach's Ouija board, out of curiosity nothing more, but The Captain had it securely tucked under his arm as he left the bar.

2 FIRST TEST - CHENNAI

FEBRUARY 20

Things are always a little tense on the day the team selection is announced. Everyone is on edge, even those who are dead certs to make the eleven. The "rotation policy" has made these announcements even more keenly awaited, with baggy greens (and match fees) hanging in the balance.

The Captain came to breakfast holding a single piece of folded paper, which he left sitting tantalisingly on his table while he went to the buffet. No one dared peak at it while he loaded up with Bircher muesli and tinned fruit. No one even dared sit with him!

The spinners were at the next table, picking at their food and talking in hushed tones while snatching furtive glances to see if The Captain was going to drop any hints their way. Nothing.

Just when everyone had resigned themselves to waiting until the ten o'clock team meeting to find out who made the cut, the Captain stood up and walked out of the room – leaving the folded piece of paper behind. As soon as he was out of sight the spinners swooped on it like a bunch of seagulls after a chip, but it was not the team list. The Captain had pulled a swifty on them, and was no doubt back in his room laughing his head off. They stormed off in disgust, leaving the scrunched up note paper fastened to the table with a bread knife.

The other players who were there casually made for the door, subtly swinging by the Captain's table so they could see it for themselves. I was last out, knowing for sure I wasn't playing, and was the last to see the single line of text that had so upset the tweakers. "Luke 12:27."* The Captain is an enigma, really.

One of the young hopefuls was in the foyer talking on his mobile. "No, haven't heard anything yet. Depends how they manage the rotation policy." His mum doesn't understand it either.

It all went by uneventfully in the end, with a simple reading of the list at the team meeting. No one cried, which was a relief. After a rousing pep talk, The Captain gave the list to the press officer, who usually passes it on to the assembled throng of journalists. The corridor outside was empty.

A lengthy net session focusing on the eleven filled up the afternoon. Only one more day of waiting until the real action starts on Friday.

* "Consider how the lilies grow. They do not labor or spin. Yet I tell you, not even Solomon in all his splendor was dressed like one of these." (Bible, New International Version, c 1984)

FEBRUARY 21

Test Eve. There's nothing like it. The Eleven and the Drinks Waiter are striding around the hotel, looking like they've got somewhere to be or something to do.

There were signs of hope at the net session today as the Top 5 started to look very comfortable against the spinners. There was no point in them facing up to the quicks, so the pace barrage got to take aim at the Reject Club. I know the Coach wants them to go hard in the three or four overs that the new ball will bounce above waist high, but man they gave it to us. I struggled to keep up the enthusiasm as the thunderbolts fizzed by, or cannoned into the fleshy parts of my person - I wasn't going to get into the team by showing the brains trust I could handle our pace attack. Not that I could.

The whole squad sweated through some fielding drills. The heat was stifling, and it was only an hour after the scheduled start time tomorrow. I hope the air-conditioning in the dressing room is working. We then had a team meeting specifically about managing the ball during the game. It's clear the only movement we'll be getting near this pitch, which looks like a slice of the Roland Garros centre court, is through the air.

The Test Squad were then whisked away for essential preparation for the Test – getting their shirts checked and audited by the Head of Sponsorship, last minute haircuts, facials and pedicures. For the five of us in The Reject Club, it really felt like the train had left the station without us. Which wasn't far from the truth – we were left to our own devices, demolishing the lunch spread the host club had left for the whole squad, and by the time we returned to the car park, it was empty. Even the autograph hunters had moved on, denying us the little bit of an ego boost we needed.

The Indian Press were finally showing some interest in the team, after spending the week camped outside Team India's training sessions. The buzz is all about whether or not this will be Sachin's last home series, so I think there's a lot of pressure on The Little Master.

The Reject Club is notorious for having a late night on Test Eve, just to squeeze some fun out of a bad situation, and to show the Twelve what they were missing out on by being selected as one of Australia's elite cricketers - a cheap night out on the slops with four other sad losers. Coach had read us the riot act, reminding us of our responsibilities to the team, and I had worked out how to get out of the hotel without him knowing, when news came through of the awful events in Hyderabad. The place filled up with security agents in a flash and Team Management were suddenly in huddles talking secretively to each other.

So, rather unexpectedly, it's a quiet night on the eve of the first test.

FEBRUARY 22
Day 1 – First Test – Chennai

The Captain called the team talk at the Hotel. Team Management (how many of them are there now?) opened with a few pleasantries until The Captain cocked an eyebrow that sent them all scurrying into the usual early morning hullabaloo in the foyer. When the big doors eased shut behind them we were by ourselves at last. Coach gave us a quick run-down on protocol, weather forecast, the ground and likely pitch conditions followed by The Captain's address at which point the eleven shoved their keep sakes deep into a spare pocket to listen for the order of battle. I will not name the player who at this point realised he was still hugging his lucky Teddy, nor where he was forced to hide it.

The Captain began in a quiet voice sweeping through the history of test campaigns on the sub-continent laced with stories of lone hands, last man stands, wounds, ties, heroism and the odd statistic just to remind us that many more promising careers have been shattered on the sparse loam of Indian pitches than have been made. Fortunately, he glossed over the story of Deano's 200 – heaven knows we've all heard that one often enough from the man himself.

Coach, with Darren's help (they seem to hang out together an awful lot), scratched out a single message on the whiteboard:

"Mental discipline.
Bat well. Bowl well. Field well. Stay alert.
Support each other
Observe the spirit of the game
WIN!

The Captain closed with a hastily constructed prayer for the opposition to bat, bowl and field poorly while eleven sweaty hands, amid the general unease, gently reached for their pockets aware of the enormity of the task before them. I've never seen so many multi-colored socks or jocks. Wicky's hoarse tones bled the team song dry yet again.

With that he held up the official batting and bowling card, fixing it to the door with a rusty bayonet he picked up in a market a few days ago. In the melee that followed, the bayonet slipped to the floor between Coach's feet. By the time he regained composure, the card lay around him like confetti. His cheek smarted from a paper burn.

My now regular paper boy threw me the TOI with the latest betting market pinned to the front page. Both predicted a grinding comprehensive win to the home side on the morning of the 5th day. No rain, no draw. I brushed up a nice note to Thea on the bus, then a punchier note to Dad to check my shares, reminding him to be civic-minded and stop kicking the neighbour's cat. I'll get a game.

The pitch was the parched dustbowl we expected with all the colour of an Ethiopian drought - a spinner's paradise. The Captain won the toss and said "We'll have a bat, mate," before anyone even blinked. A wave of relief washed through the dressing room when he made the signal sending the openers rushing off for a nervous wee.

Plopper announced "I tickled a fish once at a salmon farm in Tassie," meaning to release the stench of accumulating anxiety. A few of us in the front row guffawed, throwing open the windows for fresh air. The rest thought differently, suspending a terrified and shirtless Plopper over the side of the terrace in a three – point harness anchored by Wicky's kit.

Things were going well at lunch (2/126). Darren took the Number 1 aside to remind him that stumping is a legitimate dismissal, not to glare at the umpire as you leave the field, and to measure the distance between the crease and the top of the stands before you attempt to smash the pill into the snake charmers. On field decision-making is a fine art.

The early promise faded in the first hour after lunch. The Captain left the rooms with his heavy bat, tanked up on Gatorade, intent written on his lips. His presence reversed the momentum leading us out of the doldrums to a solid 7/316 at stumps. His prayers had been answered directly on 38, the umpire unsighted on an inside edge to bat pad. Providence rewards those who don't walk is one way to see it, and as far as the BCCI's objections to using DRS, what goes around, comes around.

The game is evenly poised. Only the spinners are making headway, threatening to unleash real venom if we lose focus.

Day 1: Australia 7/316

FEBRUARY 23
Day 2 – First Test – Chennai

The mood was buoyant on the team bus this morning, mostly because of the promise of making a decent total, but also because Darren slept in and missed the bus. Plopper noticed him running through the lobby just as the bus was pulling into the traffic, but before he could yell to the driver to stop and wait, I managed to insert a part of the team mascot into his gob and shut him up.

All the talk on the bus was about the DRS, and BCCI's refusal to let it operate in these tests. The funny thing is, given how uncomfortably hot it is, who knows if Hot Spot would even work. One wag suggested that you'd need a geologist handy on this pitch, and if there was a review they'd run out to see if they could detect any mud on the edge of the bat. Bring on Geo-Spot.

Whilst we willed the bowlers on as they scratched around in the mud with the bat, slowly building the total, it was a relief to finally get them all out of the dressing room when India started their innings. The Twelfth, still operating under the delusion that he nearly made the team, was actually paying attention, waiting to be called onto the field with drinks, tablets, hats or the latest results from Caulfield. The five members of the Reject Club got bored after the first five overs, and retreated to the coldest part of the dressing room to plot some practical jokes for the rest of the tour. Darren showed up after tea, looking like he was in need of some of his own "relaxation routines." He put on a brave face about his adventures getting to the ground. He's not much for immersing himself in the culture, so doesn't even carry any rupees in his wallet. He was very sheepish about how much he'd paid the taxi driver, but I suspect the driver's kids might well be going to college on the $A proceeds of today's fare.

The day's play finished with the game evenly poised. There is just one wicket we need desperately tomorrow, and I'm sure this will be the only subject of our team meeting in the morning. There must be a way. After all, if Pistorius can get out, so can Tendulkar.

Day 2: Australia all out 380. India 3/182.

FEBRUARY 24
Day 3 – First Test – Chennai

I spent the final part of the evening last night with the other Rejects. The degree of outright contempt Rabbit and Gipper, the outcast spinners, reserve for the selectors is quite incandescent but sobering just the same, not that I supplied anything but a sad face and a sympathetic ear.

The team meeting this morning zeroed in on The Little Master. Lord knows why. He hasn't scored a ton for 2 years. Even though he made his first ton here in Chennai, The Prof's analysis of runs per balls faced in the last hour yesterday shows that TLM has less than a 10% chance to back-up today in the same uncompromising mood. The Prof. volunteered to show Coach how to use the Ouija board correctly amid howls of laughter from The Reject Club and smiles from the Eleven.

The Captain called order. Use the same game plan as yesterday. Rotate the quicks (Rocket Man in particular), tie up the other end with spin, dismiss the little man early and domino the rest by mid-afternoon. Darren assigned seating for the bus, claiming it was to build team coherence but we all knew it was to prevent any more unseemly jostling in front of the journo's. We all clambered on regardless, the Captain's elbows working overtime. The Reject Club of course settled up the back where the Prof. pulled out two crumpled cardamom infused respirators he had made last night from spent toilet rolls to stop us gagging on the orchestral winds from the quicks on the trip to the ground. Mantis was going full bore until Lucky threatened to really put the wind up him with one of his large bats. The graffiti on the wall in the vacant lot outside the ground showing Plopper's test figures burning on a funeral pyre didn't do much for his confidence.

The locals were still streaming into the ground when play began. The same number streamed out again when TLM was dismissed, the Captain lifting his cap to the Prof. in respect.

That was the best of it. The Indian bats fired up and kept firing. Lunchtime was civil enough, with the squad washing down slabs of curried meatloaf with herbal tonics and green tea. The Captain was more animated at tea telling the bowlers, apart from Rocket Man who he really rates, in no uncertain terms that the ball was not part of the Indian space program or something you could tie a ribbon around and mail to your Valentine. Plopper was in the front row and copped most of the Captain's froth.

The game had for now slipped through our fingers. India 8/515 at the close. The Captain was pretty dark, as if anyone cared. Rabbit offered to paint a portrait of him. The Captain just stared back and told him to go and do something useful, like practicing making his stock ball turn.

The team debrief was short. Coach said it would be

better tomorrow. The Captain broke Coach's Selection Ouija board over his knees. He didn't need to say anymore. The Prof. leaned towards me whispering that the scores were similar to 2001, the double ton apart, and that the betting market was firming for a 5th day finish first hour after lunch.

Day 3: Australia 380. India 8/515 (I really had a fish on the line, Dad)

FEBRUARY 25
Day 4 – First Test – Chennai

It was a long hot day. At the end of it, all the toil and preparations had come to nothing. I came second last in the Oscars picking competition, which was won as usual by The Prof. Damn statistics of his, I don't know how he does it. I also think he had some money riding on it, and what he's made rolling that over on spreads for Day 5 is anyone's guess.

On the field, the slim hope remaining relies on the last pair getting us to a three figure lead. It also depends on being able to knock the opposition off cheaply in the fourth innings. Coach called a special bowlers' clinic after play, and this simple task nearly caused a riot in the dressing room. Plopper and Jacka had already left for a net session with the bat and Rabbit and Gipper were heading off to bowl at them. The idea that they were going to spend the next hour trying to help Plopper become a hero with the bat was galling enough, but to see a bunch of batsmen with part-time spinner delusions also heading off to practice for heroics tomorrow was too much.

Darren could see that Gipper was about to explode. He moved in gently, applied a length of gaffer tape to Gripper's mouth before he could say anything he would regret, and led the two frustrated spinners outside.

A stony silence descended in the dressing room. Occasionally it was punctuated by Puff, Mr. Bean and Hollywood groaning from the stalls, doing a little exploding of their own. The Indian Spinners were not the only thing that had ripped through the top order today. We had all been ordered to steer clear of them in case it was gastro rather than the ham and pickle sandwiches Hollywood had brought from home, and shared around just as the openers went out at the start of play.

It was too hot for the net session to go on too long. In forty minutes everyone was back in the dressing room, packing up their gear, eager to get away from the scene of today's disaster. Puff had emerged from the loo a few times, running over to his kit to put a few things away before running back to the safety of his designated stall.

Just as we were about to leave, Darren stood up and cleared his throat. "Are you ready to do something heroic tomorrow?" He mistook a loud report from Hollywood's stall as a "yes".

"Good. Let's go down to the ground and visualize the scene of our great triumph before lunch." There was another loud retort from Hollywood's stall. "Of the Eleven, those who are able, come with me."

We waited respectfully until the eight had left the room, then crowded over to the window. "This will be good," said The Prof, "last time he tried this, they ended up skipping around the boundary in formation."

It's lucky that no photos of what followed will make it back to the Australian Press. It was just too damn hot for the Hokey Pokey. Or was it a rain dance?

Day 4: Dismissed India, then took a bloody hammering

FEBRUARY 26
Day 5 – Chennai – First Test

The Reject Club took third row seats at the team meeting early, feeling smug, blameless, and expecting to see some fireworks. The Captain had been there for the last hour alone with Coach and a few of the management team he still had faith in (excluding the psycho psychologist Darren). He called us forward with his usual politeness, asking The Prof. for the odds of a miracle – rain, natural disaster, plague of snakes or boils. "We're screwed." The Prof. tapped his iPhone a few times, looking grim. "We have a better chance of winning the Ashes." He's great with numbers, not so good on tact.

The ten knew they had cocked things up. They straggled silently into the team meeting this morning like cows with bloated udders, Teddy included. It looked like the start of a Papal conclave. Coach called order. The Captain began by ripping into them with caustic one-liners he picked up from ESPN's commentary and today's TOI front page which read: "Aussie pride torpedoed by spin, again. India certain in Hyderabad". No one said anything. Ten bums wiggled around uncomfortably until they synchronised to the Captain's tapping foot. Rabbit strangled a nervous laugh, The Captain making it clear he would not get a test this side of hell if he didn't shut up. "What are you 10 going to do about it?" he yelled.

Popeye explored the benefits of cloud-seeding to buy some time, until Mr. Darcy pointed out that the local market only sold turmeric in bulk and no one had ever seen spicy rain. The Prof. said there wasn't time to seed a cloud anyway. Eventually, Jacka and Plopper offered to bat all day. Rabbit risked being sent home but managed to contain himself somehow. The Captain closed with a quick prayer.*

The team strategizing meant nothing. The final wicket fell early after play began. 241 all out. The quicks got a few overs in, just enough to avoid rotation for over-bowling, while Plopper 'worked' the other end, because at 4 for a shed load for the match, he hasn't tied up anything all game. TLM got to the crease, greeted by a gracious crowd. First ball SIX, second ball SIX. India 2/50. Game over at 10.55.

The debrief was delayed by preparations for the team after-party at a local beach rave, although it got very complicated. Coach had booked himself into a therapy centre where you strip naked, soak in a spice oil bath, and get rubbed down by two really big masseurs with arthritic knuckles. Hollywood, Popeye, and Wicky had signed up for an Ayerueda rub to balance their humours**, basically to reduce raspberries and on-camera spitting. Puff and Mr. Bean stayed at the hotel still needing to hover within striking distance of a respectable loo.

We had a few drinks with the Indian team. We tried to get away but they chased us into the car park where their simple offer of a few settlers before tonight's proceedings broke our spirits. TLM and the rest of them were at their diplomatic best sharing a few gags, rubbing shoulders with our spinners in particular as if we were family, and generally trying to rub it in.

After dark, we piled into a convoy of 8 auto-rickshaws and headed for the beach to wash away the scent of defeat. I swear we turned the same corner 4 times before we got anywhere. Coach was in a catatonic state. He lost his smile when we told him he had probably just been rubbed out with a mix of milk, bones, gallstones and heavy metals. We let him pay for the shaws and the first few rounds until his credit card maxed out.

Mr. Darcy was in his element, a lone shark in a school of slim saried beauties, deep set satin lounges, a flock of fluffy gold embroidered satin pillow things, pulsating music, peppy dances and shooters on tap. He swam off with Mr. Bean and the quicks pretty smartly. The Prof. and I surveyed all the hula gula with interest letting the cool breeze running off the ocean spice up our general mood.

The rest of the squad tried to eat elegantly with their right hands (Wicky had to take his gloves off, finally) and hold up an end with the locals. Lucky got talking to some girls from Assam or Nagarland (can't remember what he said) in the import/export business, while the rest crowded round a sweet backpacker from Brissy (who knew nothing of cricket and doesn't read TOI). The party ended when the local constabulary raided the place at 3am – no idea why, but we got out before any photos were taken.

I left a voice message for Thea and Mum letting them know I am fine and healthy. Dad had left me a short message at the hotel. You can guess what he said.

First Test: India by 8 wickets, comprehensively

Rest day tomorrow in Chennai. Considerable uncertainly about when we go to Hyderabad for Friday's Second Test.

* "Sometimes the cloud was over the tabernacle only a few days; at the Lord's command they would encamp, and then at his command they would set out." Numbers 9:20
** Air-space ('wind'), fire-water ('bile'), and water-earth ('phlegm')

FEBRUARY 27

For what was supposed to be a day off, the team meeting was a little tense this morning. Half way through a lecture about what happened last night, Mr. Darcy, wearing tell-tale sunglasses, told Coach he thought "curfew" was a migratory bird. Not a good move when it's certain that one of the quicks will be dropped ('rotated') to make way for Rabbit or Gipper for the second test. "Unless the grounds man produces a F-ing greentop!" yelled the Coach. The moment of silence that followed was broken by someone up the back whispering "I'll ring Sunil to see what odds I can get on that."

Head of Security took centre stage and gave us a full briefing about procedures while travelling to and staying in Hyderabad for the next Test. It was all rather sobering, not to mention comprehensive. After an hour and half, most were nodding or snoring deeply. His parting words were: "Lads, just remember. Indians love their cricket, which mean they love you. Stay alert!"

It seems that the exact time that we're going to head north will be kept secret until the very last minute. Apart from the request to carry our team-issued secure mobile phones at all times, we were given two very unpopular instructions, and a third made unpopular in the manner of its execution:

1) Pack up your rooms as if you're about to leave, and

2) Don't be more than 30 minutes from the hotel at any time.

Plopper seemed very relaxed about this at the time. It was only later that he found out that most of his kit did not comply with instruction 2).

3) Sponsorship duties in the Hotel lobby. Today, this meant hanging around for yet another hour, signing memorabilia for the Indian market. The Head of

Sponsorship takes this very seriously, making sure we sit in line, in order of height and sign only our own name. Misbehaving knuckles are punished with a whack from a little signature bat. A touch draconian perhaps, but fair enough after what happened on a recent tour when someone signed all 100 editions of a special commemorative team bat with the name of a player who had to leave the tour to deal with some "personal and private issues."

We dispersed for a dull day moping around the hotel. Most of the lads used the time to catch up on media commitments and social media engagements. I'm not sure what was in the video that Puff tried to upload to YouTube, but he kept the hotel Wi-Fi locked up for hours.

3 SECOND TEST - HYDERABAD

FEBRUARY 28

Hyderabad is reputedly named after a Telugu courtesan who so enraptured a local dignitary that he graced the town with her name. She must have been something special and certainly a far cry from the reality of sharing a room with Wicky. I've never seen anyone shed so much hair. The step-in shower is like a barber's shop on a busy day. I've told Wicky not to roll out of bed until he's completed 5 crossword clues so I have time to shower, dress and share a leisurely banter with the Prof downstairs over breakfast.

The bus to the ground was a creaking warship of sorts with an air-con blast like a aircraft turbine and the noise to match. Wicky sat with his precious kit on the trailer accompanied by Hollywood who said he liked to feel the wind in his hair, but really wanted some time out. There were only so many tips he could offer Lucky about playing spin before he really let loose – staying cool is his thing. I saw him from the back seat reclining, hands behind his head, Miramar sunnies on his nose, listening to

Wicky count the fingers of his gloved hands, as he watched the local sights flick past amid the black spillage of the exhaust, trading signals when the need arose with the jeep of concerned-looking Indian army regulars following on behind.

Puff and Hollywood did a few quick interviews with the Deccan Chronicle before the practice session started. Hollywood managed to describe the Chennai wicket as "really nice" (quote of the tour) and to be described as a "strapping player". Puff, whose wit was more incisive - "we need to play at our absolute [note the trisyllabic] best" – was written up merely as the "diminutive opener." Between regaling the Prof. and I with the Queen's English as he padded up, Puff let loose any residual irritation by lifting Gipper's spin repeatedly across the center wicket. This impressed the Captain but depressed the bowling staff in equal measure. Coach scratched his head.

Warnie arrived mid-session. He blew in a few days ago, expecting a call up from Cricket Australia, but has been so busy promoting a new line of aerated red jocks and eyeliners that he only met up with team management this morning. He strode into the middle of us like Ike before the D-Day landings to shed a few words of wisdom ("the tour only lasts 6 weeks" "looks like a great wicket to bat on…plenty for the quicks in the first 10 overs" "Plopper, Gipper and Rabbit are the keys"). He then stood back to reveal his new line of sweat free body shirts and rip open a bulging backpack full of red jocks. "Leftovers from journo presents boys" he said. "They snared all the Smalls and Mediums, but I figured you blokes would fit the rest. Wink, wink!". Team management dived in – stretching them, wearing them on their heads and cutting them into strips to replace The

Captain's worn jockstraps from the first Test. The rest of us stood there dumbfounded.

The Freak broke the peace. "How do you lift the seam?" at which invitation Warnie embraced us whispering his 'Top Ten Tips for Winning in Hyderabad'. It didn't matter that we'll probably read them in the Chronicle, TOI, Telegraph and SMH tomorrow. We had got them first. With a tweak of Rabbit's bum, he rolled out to instruct the Captain, Puff and the other part-timers in the finer arts of spinning on Indian wickets.

We left for the hotel at 6pm, red jocks flowing from the team kit, confident of a better show on Saturday.

MARCH 1

Last Test the team was announced a clear two days before the start of play. This time around it's all secret squirrel stuff, with the top brass meeting in corridors and broom closets. Security is tight. We seem to be under scrutiny all the time. You get the impression that some of the hotel staff might be spotting for the betting syndicates – Rabbit sneezed in the foyer last night and sent a shock wave through the market for how many runs India will win by.

The ravages of touring the subcontinent are taking their toll. While Hollywood and Mr. Bean are back to full health, Puff still has the squirts and is fading away to a shadow. The Doc has been plying him with all sorts of remedies to no avail, and is getting desperate. He even thought twice when someone suggested adding a tablespoon of Plaster of Paris to Puff's porridge just to bind things up a bit. The Prof. suggested it was all part of Puff's strategy to avoid rooming with Gipper who was getting him down. Overall, he's keeping up a brave face, but I think he lost it when he was asked to undertake a random drug test early this morning. I have a feeling the sample, while being "mid-stream", may not be pure.

With no sightseeing allowed due to security concerns, all we could do either side of the training session was consort in the Hotel gym. Hollywood settled into a gentle rhythm on the bike trying to regain some condition, listening to something on his iPod. He was so in the zone, pumping away, that he didn't notice Wicky sneaking up behind with a rubber cobra. He screamed as soon as he saw it flying straight up and off the bike. That would have been the end of it if his headphones had not splayed into the bike spokes as he dismounted. The spinning spokes plucked each little earbud off its cord sending each across the room, one striking Wicky in the eye, while the other made a bee-line to the rowing machine, striking Mantis in the middle of his bare sweaty back and sliding down the back of his shorts never to be seen again.

Wicky's precautionary scans were clear. They found nothing. The Doc said the scan was completely blank. Mantis is being airlifted out due to a virulent lower back infection. The press release called it a "training mishap". Poor Mantis. It was only last night in the bar that he said he felt good, observing that Wicky's eyes were far too close together.

The team meeting late this afternoon droned on and on. Darren was given a full half-hour to talk about mental toughness and concentration. I guess anyone who was able to pay attention through the twaddle and get through to the next level on Angry Birds has what it takes. Really, all we need is to get the quicks to get the ball to go reverse, get the spinners to land a few and for the Top 4 not to look like complete gumbies against the Indian spinners. Piece of cake!

MARCH 2

Day 1 – Second Test - Hyderabad

Over breakfast, The Prof. outlined two independent selection challenges drawing a Venn diagram on The Freak's muslin napkin to illustrate. He drew two circles next to each other in a rectangle and labeled one circle 'Bats who play spin well' and in it wrote 1-2 (+1 ret.), and the other 'Spin bowlers who win matches' writing in it 1 (ret.). He sat back in his chair with a self – satisfied expression "They'll plump for all-rounders. Bolster the batting; and pray when bowling," he said, shading the intersection between the two redrawn circles. "The betting market is now open."

The Captain read out the names of the eleven to an exam hall silence at the team meeting. The religious closed their eyes in prayer, others clutched their talisman while Puff repositioned his cork, wishing beyond hope that the Selectors had either forgiven their Chennai indiscretions or could recall promising practice game performances.

As the team was announced, the all-rounders up the back bumped chests repeatedly, snarling at the specialist quicks. The Captain reminded the eleven that the pitch would yield runs to the deserving, not the flamboyant. At that the quicks, with peachy smiles, bent forward to let go at those to the back with reverse swing. The spinners inhaled the worst of it. The complex nose of stale spices and curry sediment was like an ill wind. The place cleared in seconds, apart from Wicky who copped a knee in the face (another 'training mishap') and Plopper who had to be resuscitated in the foyer after being "rotated" out. The Prof nipped out earlier to open a trust account. He felt unsafe carrying all that cash.

Security at the ground was tight. Coach was forced to

hand in his sewing kit and crochet hook while The Captain coughed up the short handled stainless steel corkscrew he uses to test pitch conditions during play. He kept his special coin wedged between his toes.

Matthew Hayden handed a new cap to the Reserve with all the diplomacy you would expect from a colossus of the game, troweling it on good and thick amid respectful claps from the small Aussie contingent behind. The pitch looked like a geriatric, cracked in all the right places and lined with grass brasso everywhere else. India won the toss and bowled.

The Captain asked the first 4 to pad up. He did as well, first checking the weather forecast (sunny, oh joy) and that the lunch menu for the top 4 (gherkin sandwiches) was set on the rickety table in the corner of the long room. At day's end, the Prof. was off to the bank again. He felt relieved that he had managed to lay off half the bets with the Selectors.

It had been a tricky day. 4/64 at lunch followed by a recovery in the middle session, led by you know who and Wicky, who cannot remember the knee. Then a courageous declaration as the wheels fell off in the evening (5/28) just before the whole caboose hit the concrete. 9/237 declared has a nice jangle to it.

Of course, no one blames the all-rounders for failing on a specialist's wicket.

Day 1: Australia 9/237 declared

MARCH 3
Day 2 – Second Test – Hyderabad

The Artist Formerly Known as the Australian Spinner had a very long day today. It started with him showing up at the team bus wearing a purple replica of the official team Travel Strip. I have no idea how he managed to slip out to a tailor overnight, but somehow he not only did that, but also had his hair dyed black and had extensions put in to make him look like The Purple One. He was working on the sculptured stubble as well. It will be interesting to see how he rewrites the Team Song, but given proceedings so far, its uplifting passages may not be heard again until we face Bangladesh on a green-top in Brisbane.

The Head of Sponsorship normally scrutinizes the squad while they board the team bus, using his eagle eye to spot any minor infractions of sponsorship agreements. He just stood there with his mouth wide open as the A.F.K.A.T.A.S. strode straight past him in his new outfit. I checked it out during the day. Apart from being purple, it was perfectly compliant aside from the spelling of "VB."

Dad called last night. He's very frustrated not being able to see any free-to-air pictures from the tour. Being a simple kind of guy, reading what the Sydney Morning Herald has buried on page 1,324 of their new "compact" format edition is not for him. I tried to send him a link to the DC and TOI, but the whole inter-webs thing has him beat.

He made a few ripe comments about how things went yesterday. I'm dreading the next call after what happened today. All the team had to show for a whole day in the blistering heat was the wicket of an out of form opener. Apart from that brief triumph, it was none for a zillion. Plopper (aka A.F.K.A.T.A.S) just sat there watching the carnage unfold on the field. I was pleased to have the distraction of watching the catastrophe of his new hair-do unravel inevitably right before our eyes. Just after lunch, the jet black dye started to inch its way down his neck, and by tea the extensions had started to shed bits of long black hair in every direction. I don't know where he got it done, but I'll get him Kallis' email address for a recommendation for somewhere more reliable once we get to Delhi.

As the Prof. said to no one in particular with about three overs to go, "Well, that's a relief. It's not like the three best Indian batsmen are still to come." The near empty dressing room was silent in reply. He leaned over and quietly added for my benefit only: "And I've off-loaded some more bets to the English Squad."

The crowd was almost miffed not to see The Little Master bat today, but I suspect a packed coliseum will get their fill of him tomorrow. After all, the only spinner to ever bowl him is sitting beside me in the dressing room, wearing purple and looking just a little like Alice Cooper in the fading light.

Day 2: Australian 9/237 (dec). India: 1/311

MARCH 4
Day 3 - Second Test – Hyderabad

The team meeting this morning was very short. Coach looked awful, his thin hair hastily brushed, his full lips set for foul weather in the parched countenance of an aging school master teaching geometry after lunch to unruly ninth graders. He studied the team with disdain, despair, disapproval and disappointment, searching for the faintest sign of determination for a better day ahead. When he glanced to the Prof and I, chatting fitfully in the third row behind the Captain, he produced a wan smile and half-nod. His eyes had more lines, cracks and yellow overtones than a third day wicket. The full weight of unmet expectations and a dissipated demeanor seemed to have congealed all at once in his thickening jowls. "A little

Dickensian for you?" the Prof intoned, breathing breakfast on my nose. "He's close, very close. He takes it personally. It's not his fault really. It's the system," leaving me to ponder who was responsible apart from the 11.

The Captain spoke with an air of unruffled confidence, spiced by just a pinch of salt, to demand that every man play to their potential..... until lunch. That drew a few laughs from both ends to lighten the mood.

In the end, the day did have some positives. TLM lucked out early, OUTed by a third umpire referral to confirm a catch that always was - a minute's drama in an Indian summer. Only one of the centurions had scored a double ton. And after the home side slid comfortably past 4/460 in a canter, they lost 6 for 45, the Reserve and Gipper taking a brace each like it was duck-shooting season, glad handing themselves at the finish when it mattered least. Wicket-taking is all about context not figures. India all out 503, 267 ahead. Not 267, 267 ahead.

I cannot report the write-ups here in the DC and TOI or ESPN. It would do an injustice to the authors whose rich sense of Shakespearean nightmare brought it home to us in pithy one-liners that leave you gasping. Will this team be the only side ever to declare a first innings total and suffer an innings defeat? Prof. has good odds on a fifth day morning close, banking on pride to get the boys through. But I'm guessing he's also laid off some of his exposure with a few rupees on an execution by tea tomorrow.

At the change of innings, the top 4 got together to promise the bowlers they would not sweep until they had each reached three figures, or even reached it together. At stumps it was 2 down, sweeping, for 74. The bowlers had been busy on the terrace at the fall of the first wicket reshaping the spare bats of the unLucky two with handsaws and chisels. Lucky lobbed his bat on the pile when he returned, untouched as it was by leather. Rabbit threw him a new Reject Club T-shirt, for one is beyond saving when a third grader can tally your 4 innings in 15 seconds. Hollywood was heard to jest "sweeping, weeping" on his way to the middle. The Captain put aside his chisel, brushing shavings from his pads, to admire his craft work "Sweeping is for Losers". He had a serene look full of endeavour.

Wicky led the team song at the close of play. We had a light curry back at the Hotel mopped up by a stack of naan breads. Puff won't eat anything else.

Well after lights out, The Captain knocked on my door. "Get the Prof. Meet me downstairs in ten. We need to sort out a plan."

Day 3: India all out 503. Australia 2/74 (bugger)

MARCH 5
Day 4 – Second Test - Hyderabad

We were bundled out before lunch. It was shameful. The dressing room was as quiet as the crowd on Day 4 of a Shield game at the WACA. The sounds of celebration coming from the Indian dressing room were pulsating through the grandstand. It sounded like a never ending Bollywood finale, and fortunately nothing like that single that Binga put out a few years ago.

Plopper was trying not to look too smug amid the doom and gloom. He'd better be careful – there are two ways to go for a player who gets dropped before a catastrophe, and one of them involves a one way ticket to oblivion. If he gets picked again and fails to deliver, he's history. If I was him, I'd be doing a hammy at training tomorrow – Coach has already threatened that it will be a brutal session – and getting off this train wreck with a question mark rather than a cross against his name may prove a career prolonging move.

A rumour went through the squad on the bus back to the hotel that a jumbo jet was leaving Sydney tonight, loaded up with the Sheffield Shield squads of every state. According to the rumour, the Shield games scheduled for 7 March were being moved to regional grounds in India – all dust bowls – and the best performing batsmen would then be in contention for selection in the third test. A bold move by the selectors if it is true. In their already fragile mental states, the Top 4 took the news badly and were found curled up in the foetal position under the back seat of the bus. It took Darren fifteen minutes to convince them that it was all just a rumour started "for a bit of fun" by Mr. Darcy. I saw them later in a huddle in the bar, drawing things on napkins with crayons and stabbing at the table with toothpicks. Mr. Darcy had better watch his back.

When we returned to the hotel, it was nice to see that we weren't expected back yet. Our rooms hadn't been made up and there were a couple of reports of players finding hotel staff in their room rummaging around looking for saleable souvenirs of their heroes. Or DNA samples.

A team meeting was called for five o'clock. None of the eleven escaped Coach's brutal assessment of their performance. The Prof. had been foolhardy to draw fire to himself by wearing the souvenir "Turban-ator" head-gear he bought before the start of play. The Captain had to intervene as even he agreed that things were getting out of hand when Coach started yelling at the Prof. with a clinical deconstruction of Harbhajan's figures.

The official function isn't until tomorrow night, which was pretty optimistic from the off, and there's no wandering around the city given the security concerns. I hear tell there's an unofficial wake planned later in Puff's room, which I guess means he's out of quarantine. Which is at least one positive.

Second Test: India by an Innings and a Million runs.

MARCH 6

I met the Prof for breakfast early while the spread still looked pristine. My days of salvaging dirty spoons from the yoghurt bowl with the croissant calipers are over. It's a slippery business. Yoghurt ends up in odd places – that's before you have to separate it from the oatmeal dust and morsels of scrambled egg suspended where it can be eaten but not seen.

The Prof chuckled, reading from the TOI, ""Was it murder or suicide in Hyderabad yesterday?" "Listen to this one!.. Rajiv Gandhi Stadium resembled a 'cricketing abattoir' yesterday as a slew of "Australian batsmen batted like meandering Brown's cows before meeting a swift 237-minute execution"(Herald Sun)... "suicide cults have displayed more resolve" (The Australian)."

"We weren't mentioned?"

"No. Your test average is much as it was."

"That'll please Dad" I squeaked between leaves of weetbix.

"They're lambasting the four and grinding teeth over the all-rounders..."

"Maybe it's good" Darren remarked from the adjoining table, fresh as a dandelion "What else can they say if this continues?"

"Plenty"

"Interview more ex-Test stars with 50 plus averages?" bubbled Puff.

"How long have you been sitting on that?"

"Not as long as this" came the stale retort. Table expletives deleted.

"Huss said nah to a comeback...team morale down.."

"Contradicting what Cappy told them yesterday!" Everyone exploded.

The Freak joined in "Right next to a photo of the Coach with his mouth open, like he was blowing bubbles (or waiting for a banana), saying they're contemplating changes." More laughter and cracked wind ensured.

Lucky had been at the breakfast bar for a while listening to the banter. I wasn't sure what he was up to until he walked towards us to pour a mountain of creamy yoghurt, and about 5 spoons of different sizes, across the double spread of the TOI. The Prof. was mid-sentence through an engaging quote from former Test swinger Damien Fleming. He lifted his head and just stared at him. Lucky winked at the Prof. grinning. I waved Plopper away when he volunteered to help. He was more anxious to read if the TOI was floating his boat than clean up the mess, let alone confront a volatile Lucky.

On his way out the Captain announced he would bat up the order in Mohali. He is desperate to lose the 'perpetual rescuer' brand. The top four hate it.

The practice session was back at the RGS in the middle. The spinners bowled to the four all day, dropping them all over the pitch – game conditions – to draw the bats forward then back. Coach called time when the in-close fielders began to grass as many as they were catching on the shins and mid-riff. Lucky went 60 balls without touching one. The next 30 floated to the slippers. The 91st he swept to backward square. The Freak caught it one-hand behind his back. The 92nd and last went into orbit.

Puff was the first off, chasing a nasty 0-shaped stain

on his new yellow spandex. We watched his quivering cheeks leap across the browning turf as fast as he could manage it without shedding all decorum. He was last spotted crab-crawling up the steps to the sheds, two at a time, to escape a bunch of bright-eyed Indian school kids seeking autographs at the gate. Security eventually intervened, clearing a channel for the journo's to get a clear view.

The Captain pulled the Prof. and I aside clasping each of us on the shoulders to ask us how we were. There is only one topic on my mind - can Lucky's luck hold?

I spoke to Thea and Dad. Yes, I was having a good time. No, The Captain was not sending me back; No, no ex-player had accepted a call up... yet, and Yes, Shield and T20 players had all received a spam call-up from Nigeria – some had provided bank account details for debiting match payments; others had turned up at the Qantas terminal at 4am with a bank of journo's and TV crews.

4 THIRD TEST - MOHALI

MARCH 7

Today was travel day. As usual, that meant total chaos as bags were packed, checked, double-checked and loaded.

Some of the squad settle in to a hotel just a bit too much. Mr. Bean unpacks meticulously into his hotel room, and insists on discussing at length the sharing of wardrobe and drawer space with his room-mate. The trouble normally starts when he unpacks his matchbox car collection, which he takes everywhere with him. Of course, by the end of a test-match length stay anywhere, one of them has always gone missing. He interrupted breakfast today by accosting every member of the squad at least twice, asking at the top of his voice "Have you seen my Porsche?" Mr. Darcy has never roomed with him so had no idea what was going on, but yelling "I think I saw Slats driving it yesterday," was a little insensitive. Everyone knows Slats is a surfer Ferrari man.

On the other hand, some of the squad don't unpack at

all. Jacka's travel kit just sits in the corner of the room for the entire stay, slowly disgorging it's contents until it looks like Krakatoa has spewed out a mixture of clean and dirty underwear all over the room. He and his roomie spent half an hour this morning jumping on a pile of stuff in a vain attempt to squash it all back in.

More than a little home-sickness is setting in at the half way point of the tour. Some players are more emotionally self-sufficient than others and when it comes down to it, our poor on-field performances aren't helping. Very few players are receiving congratulatory emails and calls from family or friends. Lucky's Dad is emailing him a video of each of his innings, with ball by ball commentary on what he's doing wrong. At least these are short - the price the hotel charges for WiFi downloads is a killer.

Some of these jokers are just plain mummy's boys. Rocket Man is really struggling. Judging by the smell, he's a case study in how not to bring up a future test cricketer. All Mrs. Rocket needed to do was teach him how to fill out a Laundry request – honestly, it's not that hard.

The flight north to Mohali started out uneventfully, but just after take-off one of the hangers-on from Team Management was sent round with a questionnaire (24 pages!) for us each to fill in and sign about the medications and supplements we're taking. The phrase "Don't shoot the messenger!" has never been more apt. Tying him up and leaving him in the economy class toilet seemed fair enough. Honestly, this squad is squeaky clean. If anyone has secretly been on the juice, they need to change their supplier.

There's one big thing to like about Mohali – it IS cooler. Rain is forecast for late next week, which raises a serious question – are we up for a come-back, or glad to avoid the possibility of 0-3?

MARCH 8

The Punjab, the land of the 5 rivers, lies between the compass points of Nepal to the east, Pakistan immediately to the West, New Delhi to the South and the tip of India to the North. Chandigarh is tucked into the eastern border like a difficult pin placing on a par 3 green. Commissioned by Nehru in 1947, it was designed by the French architect Le Corbusier in a classic grid pattern, a drop of modernity in an old Sikh land.

I woke early to join the Prof., Mr. Bean, Hollywood and The Freak for a light breakfast. The Freak had his nose in a well-thumbed guidebook, dog-earing relevant pages as Hollywood listed a short itinerary in his elegant script. The Prof. welcomed me with a gentle wave of the hand, peering momentarily over his black-rimmed reading glasses to catch my countenance.

The squad remains in a helium cocoon confident of punishing the Indian spinners on the PCA wicket, notwithstanding the paper boy's cheeky assurance that Mohali will better suit the one-day temperament of our top 4. The drubbing in Hyderabad seems a distant memory. The cognoscenti say the series is still alive.

The Prof. set up an A-frame on the street corner this morning advertising keen odds on an Indian first innings score of 350+. It caused a near riot before 11am. Coach had the presence of mind to organize an impromptu book signing to split the crowd. He said he offloaded the Pistorius book and Darren's iPod. At the end, a disheveled Prof. had rupees leaking from his pockets, tucked under his belt and taped to his shirt. He had no idea how to close out the bets but he thought all the front-runners were selectors.

We spent a very pleasant afternoon in Chandigarh with our security detail. The Freak loved it, at home with the ramshackle hum drum, deafening honks, tailgating and hold-ups of the traffic as it eased its way between the city architecture. "Much like Buenos Aires" Mr. Bean volunteered "except newer and older," tweeting a message and a photo to his fans.

The Captain, the Prof., Hollywood and I met downstairs in the evening as planned. I'm not quite sure where we got to – it was in the country somewhere south (I'm sure we passed the Section 17 footwear outlet). We were led into a small room lit only by moonlight, adorned in flowing red and purple silks. A green parrot perched on a gnarled stoop in one corner, a belted oval wicker basket in the other. An ancient woman sat in the middle laying out taro cards with her spindly fingers. Above her dangled an old sign 'Punjab Experimental Cloning Center'. "Lucky is history" she muttered. The bird squawked "Lucky is history, Lucky is history. Ha, ha. Ha, ha." She stopped at the card of death and began to chant," The Prof. is a bankrupt, the diarist is playing! The Prof is a bankrupt. Ha, ha!"

"The diarist is playing!" the bird screeching off-key in the background.

The Captain and Hollywood laughed and laughed until they couldn't breathe. My eyes were drawn to the wicker basket which lay open on its side, a thousand cobras wrapping round my legs and slithering into my lap. I couldn't move, I couldn't move. The wicker basket lay open… #$%^!

I woke with a start lathered in sweat. The air-con was going full bore. A note had been shoved under the door. "Team meeting 7 am. Darren."

MARCH 10

I missed the team meeting and most of everything else over the weekend, felled by an unimaginably horrible stomach ache. The torrid fetid wind that came with it would put a bubbling sulphur pool to shame. I understood Puff's anguish from Hyderabad in a flash with absolute clarity. I would have gladly jumped into a pit of writhing cobras just to secure a moment's peace.

The needle the Doc hammered into my backside mid-morning Saturday felt like a blunt pile driver. I now believe the rumour that he only uses the sharp ones on the elite derrieres of the Eleven. The Doc kept an eye on me all afternoon until the sweats and hallucinating subsided. "You're on the mend. Spoke a lot of drivel about snakes, talking birds and financial ruin. If I could give all your lads a steel rocket in the glutes for mental toughness instead of flatulence I would. But spinning wickets are like wicked curries: highly destructive for the unprepared." Thanks for that, Doc. Bedside manner is not his forte, but I guess that's why he's on tour with us and not making a fortune at some cushy "clinic" in the Eastern suburbs.

Hollywood invited me to the bar tonight – soda water only. He'd been in the nets most of the afternoon. He asked me if I believed in luck. "I prefer straight drives these days," I replied, not strong enough to bear full witness to Hollywood's multi-colored socks.

I saw the Prof. later in the foyer. Wicky's under an injury cloud, again. Coach needn't worry. Wicky will be buried with his gloves on. Not to mention an eye patch, leg splint and an ice pack. Prof. didn't allude to what happened Friday night. He had spent the weekend covering his bets and currency exposures.

Back to business tomorrow - the last stand. Mohali, or

bust.

MARCH 11

What started out as a regulation team meeting this morning turned into a Quadruple Eviction episode of Big Brother. I don't think I can repeat what was said, but things were pretty tense after Coach had had his say. It didn't help when team psychologist Darren muttered "You are the weakest link. Goodbye," as the four left the room.

After the announcement was made, phones and emails were running hot. I've never heard Dad so excited. I could tell he was jumping up and down, barely able to speak, with that stupid spaniel of his barking in the background. He must have been the only person in Australia who was reacting with such joy at the news that four of the squad have been stood down for the next test for "disciplinary" reasons.

"You must be playing, tell me you're playing!"

"Dad, I won't be playing."

"Tell me you did your homework."

"Dad, I did my homework, but I won't be playing."

I don't think he was listening. But I do think it's going to be very lonely in the dressing room while the team is in the field during the Third Test. Good grief, even The Prof. has had to find his whites.

Top Eleven Best Excuses by Cricketers for not submitting their homework.

1. "I gave it to Wicky – he told me he was going to hand it in for me."

2. "Oh, I think I was absent when the homework was given out. I was certainly absent after I was given out.

Twice. Cheaply."

3. "The Team Physio ate my homework."

4. "I was too busy doing charity work at an orphanage."

5. "I emailed it to my iPad, copied it to my iPhone, and then faxed it to the hotel. Now I can't find it."

6. "Homework? I don't remember getting any homework?"

7. "How many reviews have we got left? I'm calling on the DRS. Did this homework request actually pitch in line?"

8. "It didn't come back from fiverr.com in time."

9."I left it in an auto-rickshaw after a social outing. It was a top night out, but!"

10. "I did the colouring-in section, but didn't turn the page over and see there was a written section"

11. "Things got desperate in the bathroom last night after I caught a dose of what Puff had last week. I had no option."

****

I noted down some of the top tweets from today's #HomeWorkGate scandal just for the record. A few will pass into folklore in the usual way.

@RichieBenaud_ It is very clear why Watson is upset about being banned from the Mohali Test. He has made 50% of his centuries at that ground.

@scgmacgill BREAKING NEWS: Julia Gillard stands down as PM, Mickey Arthur takes the top job. ALP sources suggest the focus was on a seamless transition.

@AltCricket Coach only asked for three points but Moises gave him ten commandments.

@rdhinds So Australia has drawn a line in the sand. An important first move for any beach cricket team.

@AltCricket #ThatAwkwardMoment when Australia became Pakistan.

@TestMatchSofa Just realised I've spent longer on Arthur's homework than Mitch, Usman, Patto and Watto put together. #homeworkgate

@AltCricket Dave Warner copied his homework off Ed Cowan.

@kokeeffe49 Australian team scorer (paper cut) and baggage manager (hand blister) are to be given to 11th hour to prove fitness for Mohali Test!!

@dmartyn30 1 thing still bothers me- how did Matt Wade play basketball but get his homework finished on time?! #teacherspet

@thecricketcouch: Homework or Work from Home #youprefer

@AresMarsFlackWatson suspended from Test team, loses pen license #INDvsAUS @FlackNews

@cmmanish Clarke suddenly has 4 less friends on FB #IndvsAus

@Testmatchsofa Do you reckon Arthur rubbed salt in the wound by showing them all Prof. Cowan's 30k word submission replete with notes and bibliography?

So @jimmaxcricket what do you call 7 blokes stood in a paddock? The Australian cricket team

MARCH 12

The 'homework-gate' volcano is spewing its red entrails high into the atmosphere, burning a smoldering gaping hole wherever it lands, whoever it touches.

Today added its own splash of raw emotion and playhouse farce. Lucky faced a torrid time in the nets, caught short ball after ball by the quicks, playing for the spin. His pads have more red splotches than his bat. The Captain took a few in the ribs from the two quicks available for selection tomorrow, looking bloody pleased or pained – it was hard to tell.

When it was his turn, the speed gun clocked Rocket Man's 6 over artillery barrage at 158 each. After the first few, The Captain cleared out, claiming 'pitch blindness'. It was hard to miss Rocket Man raising a finger for each of the bullet points he didn't submit to Coach. Prof said he'd have probably been rotated out anyway, being the best performer and all.

At the break, The Freak sidled over to the Coach to ask if he could bat at number 3. Coach looked at the smiling coconut-lathered gypsy non-plussed, mouthing a simple "I'll consider it". Puff split his sides. Darren was close by, looking confused, saddened and cross at the whole episode. Was this another team code violation, or irrepressible sardonic wit? He'd have to consult his text books, and the tea leaves.

The Captain ordered take away beef vindaloo for everyone – it was cheaper minus one big-eater. We sat at the bar downing soda water by the yard until Coach called time. He came round at 9.30 shuffling down the corridors – as if we couldn't hear him – checking for lights out

He pausing briefly at each door to listen for movement, or unauthorised fraternisation (giggling). I was reading under the covers a few minutes later when the Prof. knocked. He led me downstairs into the smiling clutches of The Little Master and two of the Indian spin trio. The homework stuff was psyching them out and they had decided to nick it! Had we seen it? No. Prof said he was in - purely to organize the betting markets and player pension fund investments for both teams - and the downside risk was low given TLM had immunity from prosecution.

Coach knew the homework was dynamite and had

taken it upon himself to protect it under lock and key, emphasizing today that he would deal harshly with any attempted theft or substitution of submitted work. He said he knew how devious we were, he did not trust us, and would be awake all night waiting for us.

The spinners distributed face masks in the image of the ex's – Gilly, Warnie, Junior, and Chappelli – while TLM signed bats for the hotel night staff. Coach was sound asleep when we entered his room, a half empty assortment of multi-coloured pills piled high in the glass on his bedside tableau. . The safe opened easily, helped by the code Coach had left under his glass of pills, to the sound of 16 pulsating iPhones confiscated during the team meeting yesterday after the "Don't Tweet, Don't Tell" policy was announced. The incoming traffic was so strong the phones were jumping over each other like cockroaches.

The homework lay underneath, 17 pages full of notes. "This will be entertaining", mouthed The Freak feet apart straddling the doorway. "I want in to the fun and the penalty. My averages and my manager can't stand the strain."

There was a stack of other notes, listed player by player in alphabetical order. I'm still going through the photocopies. We sent a few tweets to close it out, just to spike the traffic.

To add just a touch of class, TLM unstrapped a wicker basket labeled "Cobras" turning it on its side as we cleaned up. "That should keep him occupied," The Freak whispered. "Mum's the word, then."

I managed to glean the top insights from a cursory examination of our booty.

The top 3 player insights: 1) Bat better, 2) Bowl better, 3)

Field better.

The top 3 Captain's insights: 1) Sack Coach 2) Sack Darren 3) Lead from behind.

The top 3 Coach insights: 1) Sack Darren 2) Sack Darren 3) Drop Lucky, reinstate everyone else.

MARCH 13
Test Eve

What a day! The team has been in lock-down since HomeWorkGate broke. We've only seen fleeting glimpses of The Captain, Coach and Head of PR, rushing between interviews, briefings and crisis meetings.

Even though several of the squad are in need of his services, Darren has not been sighted for over 24 hours. Despite the rumours, I'm pretty sure he hasn't ducked off to Rome to take part in the Papal Conclave. If he did (he wears red robes to bed) I guess he'll be back soon.

Today's practice session was the toughest so far, with a new determination evident in the squad. The three suspended players on tour, now known as The Condemned Who Might Fire Blanks, have thrown themselves into training with gusto. The quicks gave the bats (including the Prof. and I) another bean ball work over, disappointed the Coach refused to create a formal night watchman role up the order. Mid-morning the squad let out a huge cheer as one - it appeared to the naked eye that Plopper had actually turned a stock ball.

Gipper is the only member of the squad who's a little down in the mouth. It looks like he'll be carting the drinks tomorrow, while the team is cobbled together with all-rounders and substitutes. Kerry O'Keeffe tweeted that the team scorer was in the frame, subject to a fitness test due to a paper cut. We all had a good laugh until The

Freak managed to convince our scorer that The Coach had tweeted it, which led to a very embarrassing encounter between the scorer and the Equipment Officer – a good sort.

The team won't be announced until tomorrow. I could get a run – my debut! No-one has said anything, but during lunch today one of the support staff made a joke of measuring my head with a long white shoelace. Not sure where they'll get a baggy green from – the three that were in the Coach's safe will be auctioned off for TLM's testimonial next year.

This is what I've dreamed of ever since I hit my first "four" in the Under 9s – even though the only reason it made it to the boundary was that it went straight past a kid playing with his matchbox cars in possum poo. (Mr Bean has been a worthy friend and competitor ever since.) There have been plenty more since.

But it will be bitter-sweet. You've got to be in it to win it. It doesn't matter that I might be in only because The Condemned are out of it – they'll be back, unless I can score a ton on debut. No pressure.

Forecast for tomorrow: morning showers.

MARCH 14
Day 1 - Third Test – Mohali - Part 1

Prof. and I finished reading through all the homework last night with The Freak, who kept looming up between us like a lonely albatross, his huge arms warming our shoulders like a feathered blanket. His armpit ganglia stank like a primeval bog. I reckon he wanted the team selections. Nothing doing. Prof. has them tucked away in his back pocket supporting his overnight betting market. Our replacement picks are locked in Coach's safe.

Reading the homework and Coach's comments is like

staring into a black psychological abyss. Coach's hand-written notes on each player and their suggestions show a team wracked by more than a bout of Delhi belly:

Lucky: Said he'd play better three times. He said he is lucky. Even luckier if he gets chosen, and scores a ton.

Mr. Bean: Told me to buy some decent clothes. Then he said sack Darren. He doesn't dress well.

Puff: Said he just likes to hit the ball…more often…harder. Promised to take more of the strike. Sack Darren and the girl from marketing.

The Captain: Score 400 in both innings. He is sooooooooo gracious and supportive

Wicky: Told me three times he was okay. He looked bad, hobbling out. Said he signs his name 'X'

Jacka: Promised to stay awake at team meetings. He gave me Teddy - who is full of voodoo holes and had lost an eye. Said I am a beautiful person

Reserve: Said he'll get 10 wickets and score a ton. Sack head of HR. Sack a Selector (me? The Captain?). Sack the Equipment Officer. Said he loved me.

The Freak: Axe the rotation policy.. its b/s he said. Recruit bats who can play spin, recruit bowlers who can spin – can he bowl every over? Kidnap the Selectors…its b/s he said

Hollywood: Told me in the foyer to go to 'a named School' (Hell?) and learn to facilitate adult team debriefs. He'd had enough of mashed potatoes for lunch. Sack the Doc. and see a fortune-teller

Rocket Man: Told me he regretted every joke. Wants to bat up the order. Sack Darren and the girl from marketing.

Mr. Darcy: Just wants to play. Recruit players who can hit and not get out. Sack the girl from marketing. Sack Darren. (Collusion here?)

Plopper: Told me he had adapted to India. Sack Darren and a Selector. Said he envies me but to tell the others to clean up the air.

Gipper: Promised he'll buy a few wickets late in the day. Said he feels closer to me. Feels the team is very strong.

Prof: Mentioned Mohali is his wicket. Loves my work. Sack Darren, a Selector, and the whole PR team including the girl from marketing

Other comments: Sack Darren (2), Sack masseur (1), Sack Lucky (5), Complaints about the spin bowling (many). Ingratiating comments (50)"

I took a call from Dad at first light. He'd read a blog saying I was definitely playing. He couldn't contain himself.

"Sure, it's in a team of bloody misfits, T20 wannabes and part-timers with test averages you couldn't find in a teaspoon of crack. I don't mind. A Baggy Green in our house! Fantastic!" he said.

I just tried to calm him down, check on Mum, and make sure they were including Thea.

He kept going on about the cap. "Just don't bend the cap. I hate it when Deb's do that. Everyone just thinks they're goofs."

He wanted to know who was going to present it to me. "Don't know. Hope it's Junior."

"Let me know when it is official. I'll get on a plane… hold on…(what's that racket?!)"

I'm not sure what was going on in the background. Through the ruckus I think I heard Mum say "Fred lost his job yesterday, he's at home hitting something. Now hurry up," but I'm not sure.

He wished me luck and told me again not to bend the

cap.

Better get to the team meeting on time. But it looks like rain!

Day 1 – Third Test – Mohali – Part 2

At the ground, the journo's swamped The Captain and Coach like a pack of wolves. The marketing team was busy signing autographs. Coach denied any rift between bowlers and batsmen, the Condemned and the others, players and Coach, players and The Captain and Coach, The Captain and Coach, players and Lucky, Wicky and Lucky, spinners and quicks, squad and spinners, middle order and top order. The squad was rock solid. The Test X1 would be announced 10 minutes before play.

The early morning hours ticked away remorselessly, but eventually the team was named – with good news for Yours Truly, Plopper and Gipper. Everyone was too busy playing "SuperSoaker bingo" (betting on which of the SuperSoaker drivers would be first to fall over in a puddle) to worry about presenting my baggy green. Not that I needed it – there was no play at all.

We'd been given our phones back now that the cricket, or lack thereof, had replaced HomeWorkGate in the news, but mine wasn't working properly. I found a quiet spot to make the call and, with fear and trepidation, waited to do battle with a real Indian Call Centre. The call was answered by a bloke called Brian, who sported a thick New Zealand accent that I couldn't understand. Got things sorted out eventually, eh, bro?

Coach seems to be a little unhinged, wandering around with a vacant stare. The strain of the last few days has certainly taken its toll, but I wonder whether TLM's trick with the cobra basket has robbed the Coach of precious sleep. It could have been worse – we could have been the men's relay swim team or a Code Red team of marines. As it was, he lightened up when white smoke blossomed from the Vatican – burying the remains of the last pope is a sure sign of renewal.

The Captain relaxed as the rain came down harder before lunch slapping us on the arm and tweaking the spinners' bums. He knows we're a 3-4 day side.

Being confined in the dressing room for ages like a pack of battery hens, then coming back to the hotel when play was abandoned (more confinement) is no easy feat for a team of blue blood cricketers, leaving much pent up energy ready to express itself at the team meeting this afternoon. Darren spotted it, and took center stage after The Captain's pep talk.

"OK, boys, let's do a few stretches and let out some of that nasty tension. Stand up, move the chairs out of the way," he said, flicking his wrists this way and that.

Then he said "Now, find a partner." This kind of thing always ends badly, as the competitive nature of an elite sportsman is never far below the surface. We started with a few arm stretches, but when it came to pushing against each other, things turned ugly. Darren was going "Ready, Set, Go" slower than a Rugby ref does "Crouch, Touch, Pause, Engage." Rocket Man got impatient on "Set" and in three steps had slammed Plopper against the wall, winding him on impact. Mr. Darcy was about to take the strain from a muscled-up Puff, but stood aside at the last minute allowing Puff to rocket through the room like a rhino on heat, crashing into a pile of table and chairs under the weight of his own momentum. The Captain called an immediate halt to proceedings. All we could see as we left for dinner were Puff's little legs up in the air, kicking about madly.

More showers are forecast tomorrow morning, so let's

see what we can do in three and a half days.

MARCH 15

Day 2 – Third Test – Mohali

"The forecast is fine. We'll start on schedule" the Coach concluded. Just do it!" was the command I remember.

As the bus trundled to the PCA ground, anxiety smothered me more than the methane cloud from team management, who had formed a gym-tuned flying wedge to batter their way to the front seats. The somber mood of the XI helped steel our collective resolve to bury HomeWorkGate and get on with the business of winning. The Prof. thought it more to do with the heady pall from the front, tinged as it was with The Captain's French cologne ('Pour les Hommes') and the gritty aftertaste of motor diesel.

The twitter traffic was all positive – even Lucky had some support from a group of child psychologists in Dunedin.

Junior did present me with my test cap. I can't remember what he said it was so brief. The marketing girl said it was witty, willing and wonderful (I think she likes him!). There were more grins, laughs and bum tickles than a medieval theatre. The Freak even bent my cap for me.

Team management played a tape of a roaring Melbourne crowd from the '70's over the ground PA at the end, muffling the few claps from the ground staff and a half nod from TLM looking on from the Indian dressing rooms. Nice.

The openers got off to a breezy start when play began, the first time on Tour we had been in such an impregnable position at the start of Day 2 - 130 odd without loss at lunch. Coach finally cracked a smile, and a tiny righteous breeze, no doubt convinced that homework breeds 'form'. He kept this golden nugget to himself.

The Prof. was busy running a Monte Carlo simulation on innings scores, keen to offer sensible odds on scoring 50 and a ton on my debut. I harbored vague thoughts on batting late in the day for an instant before the rot set in, something called 'mean reversion' that left the game tastily balanced at 7/273 at stumps.

The Captain was happy enough despite his first ball duck. The Freak studied him with the binoculars as he walked off, as unperturbed and purely white as when he walked on. He could have been a Jesuit. But The Freak knew better. "He's boiling with acid boys. He's got that false Mona Lisa half-smile stuck solid for the cameras. There's no way he'll take his helmet off." A bunch of IOU's changed hands in a twinkle. "Quick. He's stopped to say something to Lucky." Half a dozen binoculars focused on the short exchange. "Lucky looks a little put out."

"No, no. He's cool". Everyone knew The Captain's average is no better than Lucky's when batting at 3. A true Captain's innings – taking one (or in this case a zero) for the team.

Lucky was back by the time The Captain had showered. "What are you doing here?" he said, resting a caring hand on Lucky's shoulder and nodding to Darren who guided him away discreetly for a quick one-on-one.

"The fortune-teller was right," tweeted Mr. Darcy. "Lucky is gone."

Then it was my turn. Prof. said it was about 80 steps to the middle. I needed to pee, badly. I was sweating like a thoroughbred just as Mum said. This was it and I didn't have a clue. The first ball spun so far wide I just watched it. I think I saw the second hit the bat between the moon dust from the pitch as I was called through for a quick single. End of the over!

Jacka reminded me mid-pitch that the game is to get off strike by scoring runs. "Relax. No one's watching." I looked around. The ground was empty. Who could blame them?

Jacka stayed long enough for me to pass on the betting market. Somehow I was there at the close, the pitch throwing rubbish in my face, surrounded by a ring of hopeful catchers and a spinning ball that had seen better days.

Day 2: Australia 7/273 (hopeful)

MARCH 16
Day 3 – Third Test – Mohali.

It's hard to believe how far you can fall in one day of cricket. The mood at lunch today was amazing – like we'd just won the Ashes - such was the relief at having made it past 400 on the strength of a couple of notable nineties. Racking up 400 in the first innings of a rain shortened match should mean that a draw is the worst possible outcome that awaits.

By the end of the day, all our notable achievements - mainly mine, of course – were being swept around the empty stadium with the chip wrappers in the breeze, blown away by the Indian openers. If only one of the Condemned had done their homework on the subject of "Not letting Dhawan become the new Sehwag in one innings." Nothing we tried worked, especially telling The Captain that Rocket Man should be bowling. He knew that already. Stemming the flow of runs on this pitch was about as difficult as poking a cat out from under a verandah on a rainy day with a wet piece of rope.

The dressing room at the end of the day's play was so quiet we could hear Prof's brain ticking over, trying to work out what exposures he'd have to lay off over night. No-one had to say it, but everyone knew it. If India bat like that tomorrow, then declare at the end of the day 200+ ahead, we could be in for a sticky time on Day 5. The Condemned had concerned looks on their faces, but I bet they're glad they're not in the frame for adding another "snatch defeat from the jaws of victory" to their resumes. You can't say that The Reject Club didn't step up. Apart from Gipper, who had a shocker. Comment of the day went to Mr. Bean: "Well done, Gips, you've perfected that straight ball!"

On the way back to the hotel, the mood lifted a little thanks to The Freak, who reminded us of the team tradition when a player gets out on 99. I kept quiet through the whole thing – I certainly wasn't volunteering my razor, my secret stash of golden syrup or the contents of the feather pillow I've been carrying around with me all this time. I don't know why Rocket Man has 99 Luft Balloons on his iPod, but it was on at full volume all the way back to the hotel.

There were three team meetings tonight. Three! I didn't hear a word. I just sat there, dreaming of what might have been, seeing the Ump's finger in the air.

Dad's email was short. "Bradman never got out in the 90s while going on 29 times. Mind you, Slats did it nine times, and you only once. Well done, son."

Day 3: Australia all out 408. India 0/2,830

MARCH 17
Day 4 – Third test – Mohali
Coach and Warnie facilitated a structured '6 Thinking

Hats' discussion this morning over breakfast on the topic "Dismissing the Men in Blue". The squad split into genome profiles: bats, ball-ers (sub-profile spinners), and Rejects. Team management sent an apology – they were at a spin class. When we finished, the front wall was covered in multi-coloured post-it-notes. Warnie then expertly re-arranged them as a twin pair of floating jocks, drawing on his recent study of pointillist painting in Paris, just to hold our interest. According to the flyers on our seats, his new briefs had taken hold, prompting him to deliver monographed packs of ten to each of the Men in Blue.

After much discussion, he labeled the first pair 'Seriously'. 'Seriously' was conventional yet seemed to shape like a sine wave with a higher thigh cut and deeper slung trough. I took this to mean greater certainty of outcome yet more difficult for the XI to execute. The green and white notes were brief, exhorting the bowlers to lift it, swing it, cut it, spin it, catch it and leg it. The red and black splotches in the trough showed no one was up to another wicketless session. Not even our entourage. Yesterday, the press reported spikes in call center traffic at the PCA ground from our partners and girlfriends to check income protection policies and disability payout rates.

The second pair labeled 'Man Overboard' contained the X factor fueled primarily by witticisms from The Freak, Mr. Darcy and The Reserve. Apart from unsettling the Men in Blue with a really hot samosa, tampering with their kits or the ball, using more subtle psychological terror (sledging, shadowing, mankading, underarming) or tossing real pies, nothing excited our imagination. The consensus view was depressingly conventional. No shortcuts, haircuts or off cuts. Just bowl well and bat better.

"Is that it?" Puff mumbled. "Don't think 400 is 'high performance'. It's 800 on this pitch" Coach shot back. The rumble was on after that. Coach emerged at various points trying to get Darren's attention, his shirt in tatters, before he was sucked back into the melee. It ended as quickly as it began, by my reckoning as soon as Coach's pink boxer shorts saw the light of day. The Captain blew his whistle, leading the team onto the bus single file, in the right pressed strip, with not a word to the underage journo's or the paper boy they were hounding for a quote.

Airing team grievances seemed to work. India was skittled for a comparatively modest 499, TLM, MSD and the spin stable put in their place by simple steady bowling. The Freak shared the applause at the change of innings. His new Bobble Ball (a combo doosra, carrom, in-swinging, out-swinger slider) that he crowd-sourced via the paper boy at the Hotel seemed to do much of the damage, although it was clear that the bowlers had all worked hard to give Lucky plenty of game time early in the second dig.

The dressing-rooms were chock a block between showering bowlers trying to slip soaps into spare kits and the top 6 padding up, while waves of dirty water sloshed underneath like a Newfoundland tide.

The Captain had been off earlier – a 'back complaint' – as a result of which he was 'unsuited' to bat at 3. Lucky struck pay dirt at long last, managing to cheat the percentages to score healthily behind the wicket for a breezy 50. The Men in Blue led by the man with the 'tash' and 'the fastest deb test century' made an honour guard to celebrate. He came off the ground smiling uncontrollably like a Cheshire cat. The dressing-room door was locked and boarded up. A sign, hanging by a rusty tack, read "Too late". We were giggling inside with party hats, cupcakes and balloons expecting a bit of fun. It scared the devil from us when he strolled through the barred door hands apart as if he walked on water. The Freak said he looked like KP, the English firebrand and essayist.

The Prof. has worked out how to use the skin fold calipers. We should get a sensible result for this test.

Day 4: Australia 408. India 499. Australia 3/75

MARCH 18
Day 5 – Third Test – Mohali

The match limped on to the inevitable result, with a slight hint of drama near the end masking the fact that we had managed to throw this one away in under 4 days of play. It was much like watching a barrel full of precious cargo roll gently over Victoria Falls. You know it will be smashed to bits on the rocks below, but you hope like hell it won't all the same.

Coach was encouraging when we came off, saying we fought well at the end. "Pity about the start and the middle," Prof. said under his breath. He took his whites off and scrunched them up in his kit. "No point in even having these washed. The Condemned will all be back in next match. Where's that Reject Club t-shirt?"

The LBW stats for this series are a bit mysterious, given how many straight balls Plopper and Gipper have attempted to slip in. One thing the umps haven't said to either side is "spinning too much". Make of that what you will.

There is a rumor going around that no one has been able to get a business class seat on a flight to anywhere near Delhi for days. The Condemned Who Is Not Firing

Blanks is on the way back with his entourage, which will be a relief to us all. Apart from that, apparently every player who thinks they're on the fringe of test selection, and is not playing in the Shield final, is trying to get to Delhi so they can send the selectors an email saying "I'm here on holidays if you need me." The only thing that prevented an unseemly rush to Sydney airport at the end of the Blues v. Redbacks game was that the game finished early, so the Blues players had to wait until the other games had finished to find out if they had done a Bradbury into the Shield final. That and the fact that their fringe players are already in the squad, me included.

I guess one thing we can be thankful for is that there are no pollies on their way over here to catch a publicity shot with us being presented with the Border-Gavaskar trophy. They won't even be sending a junior ministerial assistant to the airport to meet us at this rate, unless their polling indicates a large degree of sympathy for us among swinging voters in marginal seats. Judging by the emails and chat on twitter, there would be more votes in gleefully dancing on our graves.

No-one is game to say it out loud, but there is a feeling that this was as close as we're going to get, on a pitch that gave just a little help to the quicks, notwithstanding Rocket Man's detention. Back to playing in dust on Friday by all accounts.

Third Test: India by 6 wickets (demoralizing)

MARCH 19

Losing a third test match (or falling just short, again) by six wickets at the end of the 4th day of play, when you score 400 by midday on Day 2, is hard to fathom. I expected harsh words from home this morning and was not disappointed. Dad accused me of swinging the bat like a fairy's wand spraying curry dust everywhere to no effect, an opening salvo in what became a Shakespearean soliloquy that contained all the spice but none of its linguistic tenderness.

"You are in the Australian side, son. It's a badge of honour YOU need to take seriously…"

Thea was friendly, but cool. Even non-cricket lovers expected better.

The Freak said this is rock bottom. "The GFC we had to have". His Dad has refused to speak to him despite his 5 fer.

Gipper reckons you can't understand it unless you are playing. His Dad sold up yesterday and moved interstate. He lost it when a load of old cricket balls was dumped on the front lawn overnight. The pyjama wearing crowd that congregated at daybreak looked like the second day of a marathon petanque festival. Mum fronted the journo's who turned up later to say her son was a great boy, really. That was the last straw.

Everything considered, the mood in the camp is very up-beat. As The Captain reported, there are many, many positives. We can take a swag of wickets (9/200) when the pressure is off. We just need to bust the 250 run partnerships early on. The Condemned have been freed. Lucky is back scoring well through slips. And it's the year of the Snake.

Coach offered his analysis of the match at the team meeting, to which we listened attentively because we love him. He kept it brief recognising that the bell for recess was about to go. "Bowlers scoring more runs than the top 4, again. Top 4 wanting to bowl, again. Spinners taking no wickets, again. Only a few oil patches amongst a sea of positivist plenty", he said. "Oodles to work on before Delhi." Coach released the marked homework. No surprises here. The Captain failed and had to write 100 lines about gold and ducks, which he delegated to Hollywood – after all, that's what the Captain's aide is for - as he raised his hands like Caesar for quiet. He had received a note from MSD requesting us to join the Indian team for afternoon drinks. Knowing this might be a sensitive point, he wanted our views. Were we up to it? No unease at all – all proper smiles and breaths of wind.

Drinks was an elaborate affair. The Indian top six had showered and were in engaging spirits titillated no doubt by the prospect of slipping in a few kind words amid the diplomatic chatter. Dharwan talked us all through his 3 or 4 balls of nervousness before he got into his natural game. "I was in no hurry" he smiled, swinging a hand around Puff's waist "no strategy…I was just middling it." Puff smiled back, a hand around a shoulder. "I'm in no hurry either. How is your hand? Can I show you how to dive properly?"

Across the room, The Captain and MSD were deep in conversation, MSD very animated as he explained his approach to homework. "I drop the work bit," he said. "It's still about respecting your home, your honour, your sponsorships, respecting your boss and his boss's boss… When we lost 4-0 in Australia, the homework was only to find a faster way home. We also placed calls to the pitch curators. The BCCI did the rest organising as many tests here as they could to let our averages recover. Cricket is a big industry. It's a 20 year career here. TLM is still a brilliant Harvard case study. I see your spinners and ours are talking again", pointing to a gathering of 6 on the patio. "There are no secrets in our camp. Spinners learn to spin on hockey pitches; bats learn to bat with a ball and stump," he said winking.

The Prof. and I occupied our time moving in and out

of these conversations, Prof. taking bets mainly from the Indian spinners on behalf of MSD and the top 6 (TLM apart) on the prospect of a 4-0 sweep, prompting another security-escorted trip to a local bank. As the hazy sun began to dance above the Chandigarh skyline – to be frank we were all at that stage - The Freak and I nipped away to put our finishing touches to the Indian bus with spray paint, animal glue, and a bunch of tacks from the hotel boy. There is nothing like revenge.

5 FOURTH TEST - DELHI

MARCH 20

The phalanx of physios looking after the team has been bolstered by three new arrivals from Australia, who were waiting for us when we arrived in Delhi. The Prof. has a theory about why they are dressed up to look like Bob Kater, but he refuses to share it with me.

A round-the-clock roster has been scheduled to work on the Captain's back - he hasn't been off the massage table since we got to the hotel, apart from fronting a news conference to say he was hoping to be right to play.

It seems natural that the existing Vice will captain the team if needed, but the whole issue of who will be playing in Friday is still up in the air. Given that the Reject Club performed with some distinction when they were selected to replace The Condemned in Mohali, the manoeuvring to impress the Captain (who's horizontal) and the Coach (who is trapezoidal) in their capacities as selectors is on in earnest. Gipper in particular is running an enthusiastic campaign, but Prof. is pretty sure he won't get enough votes to get his deposit back. The team spirit has improved, although individual insecurities are much more evident. The Freak has no worries about his spot in the team, but Mr. Darcy, Mantis and Rocket Man have worked out (The Freak must have told them) that there will only be two other quicks in the team and each of them has a 50% chance of bagging a spot.

This good natured competitiveness is being exercised on the batsmen in the practice nets - I've got the bruises to prove it. Lucky was cut in half by what the late and great Tony Greig would have called a "norsty delivery". It took half an hour for the physio to reattach his torso with the magic spray and calm him down reminding him that qualifying every noun with the same word to describe his anguish and his friendship with Mr. Darcy could be seen as frustration. Lucky refused to resume his net session until his parts had been subjected to several ice therapy immersions in the sheds. It is likely that there will be no proceedings in that region of his anatomy for some time.

When we got back to the hotel, I passed one of the physios in the hall. He was off to have a break, rubbing his throbbing muscle-bound digits, having been subbed-off duty on The Back. Trained not to give anything away under scrutiny, he was stony faced, but I did manage to get him to confirm that, unlike in Canberra, there were no knives in the Captain's back.

Test Eve tomorrow. Something has to give.

MARCH 21

Test eve - Delhi

> "Said I one night to a pristine seer
> (Who knew the secrets of whirling time)
> "Sir, you well perceive
> That goodness and faith,
> Fidelity and love
> Have all departed from this sorry land
> Father and son are at each other's throat;
> Brother fights brother, Unity and federation are
> undermined
> Despite all these ominous signs,
> Why has not Doomsday come?
> Who holds the reins of the Final Catastrophe?"
> Mirzah Ghalib (Urdu Poet 1797-1869)

The fortune-teller uttered not a word more, lapsing into some sort of transcendental union. "An Urdu poet...what the hell does that mean?" whispered Rocket man. The Prof. pushed his cap back across his curly mane "4-0 for sure", thinking harder about the overnight message from his banker than unraveling hidden forebodings from a long retired mystic. "I'm more comfortable with the steady meter of Shakespearean sonnets" Puff incanted as they left. The cool night air stilled further banter, wrapping each of us in our own thoughts.

The team meeting late in the afternoon focused on the three C's: Commitment, Capability and Composition. Commitment to winning 15 sessions; Capability to carry net form to the middle (of the bat) and Composition to "swim between the flags" – don't do anything stupid before you get to 10 or at any other time. The Captain then gave an update on his back. He could balance on his midriff like a rearing cobra – at this point Coach's temple started throbbing as if in nuclear alert – but he was not sure if he could bowl. We oozed sympathy for Hollywood, given the obvious bulge in The Captain's back and obfuscating press references from team management about his form and leadership capacity.

The unnatural parallels to Australian events add spice to the pre-Test tension. Four Condemned have been relegated to the back bench awaiting reinstatement, the incapacitated Leader is protesting good health although she has more knives in her back than a fifth day pitch has cracks, and The Future (an accidental tourist?) is leaning against the pillars of September to catch up to the past. Is this a vision or a waking dream?

Hollywood wrapped up the session leading us in solemn prayer. As befits this city, which has been ransacked and rebuilt so many times over the last 2,500 years, he paid homage to every form of religious devotion. It was evensong by the time we finished rubbing our eyes and reinvigorated our pulses, as Coach cleaned up the Ouija board which had a thick join where The Captain had broken it early in the Tour. We joined shoulders moving in and out in a square dance, knocking hips, elbows and the occasional head to the martial cadences of the team song.

The Prof walked out with Gipper, arm in arm. Gipper clearly had been holding something back. "This reminds me of King Lear Act III, Scene II." "Huh,… yes. Indeed!" Prof replied recalling the scene "'King Lear, with the Fool, in a storm'." The bowlers behind guffawed adding a slight tailwind to Gipper's spirited recitation:

"Blow, winds, and crack your cheeks! rage! blow!
You cataracts and hurricanes, spout
Till you have drench'd our steeples, drown'd the cocks!
You sulphurous and thought-executing fires,
Vaunt-couriers to oak-cleaving thunderbolts,
Singe my white head! And thou, all-shaking thunder,
Smite flat the thick rotundity o' the world!
Crack nature's moulds, an germens spill at once,
That make ingrateful man!"

The Captain, Hollywood, and Puff, a media scrum in tow, went to the Ferozeshah Kotla to inspect the wicket declaring it to be a typical weary end-of-season dust bowl with more under-surface fissures than a hot springs – "a fine batting wicket for three days" Puff was reported to say. "Do you support Hollywood" a precocious reporter fired "Unreservedly. On my honour" spoke The Captain.

One thought occupies Prof's idle mind: Can we win at the Kotla? I imagine the Leader is praying for rain in September as much as Coach is praying The Captain is fit to play tomorrow. Frankly, I put more store in the pocket-sized anthology of Ghalib's poems I picked up at the bazaar.

MARCH 22
Day 1 – Fourth Test –Delhi

The Bob Kater look-alike physios were putting it away at breakfast this morning, and I assumed that meant they'd been up all night working on The Back. Prof. was looking very nervous, and not about whether he was going to be playing today. Maybe he hasn't been able to cover an exposure here or there overnight.

In the end, the Captain was out of the team due to a

non-homework related back issue. That meant two things. Hollywood would be filling in the team sheet (Mr Bean helpfully offered to sharpen his crayon for him) and I would be getting another Test. Does that make me a two-test veteran, or, as someone in the press corps said, the owner of the Baggy Green least likely to wear out from over use?

Hollywood kept the run of successful calls at the toss going, and really, that was all that was required of him apart from scoring some runs. Instead, he did a cartwheel in celebration on his way back to the dressing room, ripping the arm off his team blazer. When he stumbled a bit on landing I thought he might have ripped his ACL as well, but he was fine.

As far as the cricket goes, it was not a good day. There were several low scores, and of those who got a start, only The Freak managed to make it to 50. Twitter has been alive with the idea of reversing the batting order based on form, and today will give more fuel to that preposterous proposition. I'm kicking myself for getting out just shy of a 50 after working so hard, something Dad hammered home when he rang while I was still at the ground.

We were back at the hotel when my mobile rang again. I answered it without thinking – there wasn't anyone I really wanted to talk to anyway. It was Brian the New Zealander from the call center at the telco that Warnie recommended. We'd talked about cricket when he fixed up my phone last week, and at first I thought he was just checking up on how things were going with the phone. But no, he was ringing up to gloat about how well the Black Caps were going against England. "We were sent in and got 1 for 250 on the first day. How did you guys go?"

I didn't want to engage, but I guess our 231 runs was

okay if you didn't count the wickets. Then I thought he said "It was fun taking no wickets that made the difference." I was about to ask him if they were batting or bowling, but it was obvious something was lost in translation. I'm sure Finn will strike back tomorrow.

As we need to.

Day 1: Australia 8/231

MARCH 23

Day 2 – Fourth Test – Delhi

The Captain left for the airport early flanked by Darren and Coach, and a ministerial entourage of injured masseurs trailing ribbons of antiseptic gauze from bandaged hands and swollen arms.

Hollywood called for quiet as he announced a new policy of on-field communication for Day 2 that unleashed a storm of wild approval from the Rejects, the Mohali 4, and some of the more outspoken regulars. The ruckus drowned out the few squeals of protest from team management at the back. As the marketing girl distributed heavily thumbed copies of the Thesaurus and Brewers Dictionary of Phrase and Fable, drawing attention to highlighted one-liners for those wits with thespian pretensions, Hollywood read purple passages from Steve Waugh's annotated supplement to the Art and Rules of Cricket. "A good session sledging pattern plays with a batter's conscience and to the crowd. The object is to add tension usually with oblique references to anything that irritates. Tension takes wickets."

The squad repaired to the pool for an hour to get in the groove, while the marketing girl sat in the shade with a floppy hat reworking tame one-liners ["(…), if you turn the bat over, you'll see the instructions on the back"] she suspected the players would sideline for their own simple vocabulary when play began.

The ground was buzzing when we arrived, salivating at the prospect of a 500+ Indian total at stumps featuring a last hurrah at Kotla for TLM. It looked that way at 2/130 when things turned for us on the back of news at the drinks break that the Indian Badminton team was short 50 barrels of shuttlecocks due to a ministerial import ban imposed during the avian flu scare. The Freak related this to the Indian pair with some adjustment and familial reminders that continued when play resumed.

Wickets continued to fall. Plopper jagged 5, acknowledging each with the type of unique 'how's your mother' salutation most confidently given when you are surrounded by 10 really tall strong blokes devoted to your well-being. Ribald send-offs like that rebound in your skull like a pinball machine every step to the gate. Plopper was like an Irish setter off his leash – sniffing for the next wicket, howling appeals to anyone who would listen egged on by Rocket Man and The Freak.

Puff took offense after some banter with Vijay backfired – I think he tried one of the marketing girl's one-liners – and Vijay offered him his bat. The crowd, sensing the amusement, began to chant "Loser, loser, loser" at us. It didn't matter. All the chatter combined with unplayable scooters and rib ticklers unnerved the Indian bats for the first time in the tour.

At least this is what made most sense until I learned that the Indian team and a billion of their supporters had bet big on a fourth test massacre which threatened the stability of the global capital markets and the US debt ceiling. The prospect of losing big on a match you are meant to win upsets your radar much more than quick quips about your mother and a few barrels of feathered shuttles.

Day 2: Australia all out 262. India 8/266.

MARCH 24

Day 3 – Fourth Test – Delhi

It's hard to know whether or not to be relieved that it was all over so quickly. Even though there were brief glimpses today of how we could have won a consolation Test, each time they were snuffed out by a rampant India – with the ball, and then with the bat.

In spite of the on-field heat yesterday, the Indians were very magnanimous to invite us to their rooms at the end of play. It was a real eye opener – the visiting team dressing rooms had been good enough, but the home team rooms were palatial. The BCCI had obviously decided to reward the players with a big celebration. It was like a Bollywood set in there, with wild dancing and music - MSD told Hollywood this was just the warm-up act and urged us to stay longer. Even the stand-in Captain knew we could only take so much force-feeding of humble pie, leading us away after a polite few drinks. We really needed to lick our wounds in private. The ground staff knew this and thoughtfully refused our bus entry into the security area. We had to drag our sorry arses and kits out past the celebrating crowd – who let us know who had won the contest with a solid round of chirping and flamboyant hand gestures.

Call Centre Brian was on the phone again. "How's the cricket looking for tomorrow? I haven't seen the score…" he lied. I humoured him with "We'll be pressing for a win. How about the Black Caps?" What was I thinking? He fired back with "Pretty much the same. 274 in front, 7 wickets in hand. England don't have KP for the chase, and Boult has the ball swinging around like a dunny door in a Wellington howler. We're doing our best to soften them up before the Ashes. Anyway, best of luck."

It looks like I might be stuck here until Wednesday – the flights were all booked months ago by someone who was wearing the rosy coloured glasses that made them expect the last test to go 5 days. Even if they can arrange the tickets, the airline won't have had a chance to stock up with the supplies they need to keep us well lubricated on the long flight home. Under normal circumstances, there isn't that much VB in the city, but with most of the squad staying in India for the IPL, they should be able to arrange something.

I've been appointed to the committee tasked with nominating the team awards for the end of tour dinner tomorrow night. There's a fine line to walk between having some fun together and rubbing a poorly performing team member's nose in the fact that their career may be over. That will keep me busy all day tomorrow.

I got back to my room late. All I wanted was to have a long shower and wash away the dust. Sitting on the bed was a plucked shuttlecock. Must have been Kohli – a good effort, I must admit. I picked up the plucked bird, pulled the curtains aside and threw it out the open window. It sank like a stone into the courtyard below. I looked out to see it wasn't alone.

Australia 262 and 164. India 272 and 4/158.

India by 6 wickets.

India 4-0

MARCH 25
Day 4 – Fourth Test – Delhi

The Prof and I breakfasted early as usual. The Prof

looked considerably refreshed, keen to relate how he managed to rescue his betting empire from ignominious collapse barely 48 hours ago. India was an unbackable favourite last Friday. Things were well under control until the hotel boy the Prof had recruited in Chennai reset the odds at 20:1, backing in his parents' savings and his uncle's trucking company for a modest tax free windfall. In one hour, before the Prof found out and closed him down, the lad had accepted USD$700Bn in bets from farmers in the Punjab, Saudi Sheiks, Gerard Depardieu (from his Siberian chalet), Chinese construction companies, and the Bank of England – anyone and everyone.

The Prof said his bankers went crazy when they realised they had guaranteed his liabilities after the Chennai Test to the end of the Tour as full partners in the No. 1 Fund. "If I wasn't part of the Squad I would be roasting by the Ganges" he said. "But they couldn't touch me for fear of ending the Tour and losing everything". The bankers paid S&P and Moody's to rate these bets AAA, off-loading them as MBS mark IV into Cyprus, the PIGS, and to California renters saving to re-buy their homes. Another group sold them forward to the new breed of young guns desperate for a mid-year bonus.

When the music stopped and everyone figured it out, Cameron lit a fuse in the UK and the FDIC had a minor meltdown. "Worse than a front bench walk out," I stammered, a little confused.

"The only way to balance the books was to reverse the cycle, savers borrowing from their banks and so forth, backed by a balancing bet on Australia to lose on the fourth day, a complex conditional probability problem offered to the same punters at 25:1″

"As reasonable a bet as one could imagine at the end

of Day 2... "

The Freak joined us, hair adrift, disheveled and sleep deprived, when the Prof left, leaving me to ponder who was in control of this Tour - the players, the Coach, Team Management, the hotel boy, or the Punjabi farmer.

The Prof, Rocket Man, and I walked the streets of old Delhi in the afternoon steadying ourselves for the traditional end of Tour Awards dinner. The evening went off without a hitch. AB was the surprise MC. He never submitted homework during his career he said through a cheesy grin, the first of many one-liners he pumped out between drinks and the awards ceremony.

I recorded the awards on the back of Plopper's dirty napkin.

Batting
The Bowlers' Batsman Award: Mr Darcy, highest almost ton (99).
The Captain's All-rounder (joint): The Freak "only Australian batsmen cannot bat in India", and Jacka "only bowlers can bat in India."

Bowling
Most injuries caused: Rocket Man "I bruise batsmen, ours and theirs."
Most wickets: Plopper "At my best in long spells when the game is beyond reach" Ripples of polite applause.
Most Expensive Wickets: Mr Darcy, "I should bat at 4."
Most pies: Gipper "These wickets don't take spin."
Bowlers' Award to Batsmen: "We prefer to bowl with a new ball, not face it. Do your homework."

The Golden Hand Award: Wicky "I caught the one's that really mattered."

General

The Players' Player Award: Rabbit (wild cheering and kisses), the only player not to play a Test.

The Bunny Award: The Captain, scalped 5 times by Jadeja. Plenty of guffawing from the XI.

The Global Capital Markets (GCM) Award: Prof, for the largest intra-day rise in the UK 10yr bond rate since 2007.

The Wisden Statisticians Award: Lucky, most balls faced and wickets lost without scoring a run (not even a sundry).

The Indian Hoteliers Award: Puff, most sandwiches eaten in 60 seconds at an official team function (10).

The Chirper's Award for the Best Send-off: Plopper, for using the same word thrice in one mouthful.

The Chirper's chirping Award: Rocket man "I read Shakespeare a lot."

The Brass Bands of Australia Award (by telephone): Puff, loudest report in a public place.

Most Annoying Roomie Award: Mr. Bean's matchbox Leyland P76, for crawling up Ploppers inside leg at 3am.

The Coach's Award: Darren, for his paper 'Swimming Between the Flags: Batting on the Subcontinent under the Influence of Equine Stimulants.'

The award ceremony was suspended for 15 minutes while security restored order. The girl from marketing found Darren in the back stalls, his award stuffed in his mouth next to a few lines scrawled on the wall in red lipstick. "I'd do anything for a few days off, but I won't do that" groaned Darren. She added her own artistry before tying his shoelaces together. "Mum's the word".

The place was held at fever pitch (and a round of drinks) for the final most prestigious Tour award

The Times of India Award: Coach, for the best Coach to Tour India since 1984

After that we all broke wind in time to Sgt. Pepper's Lonely Hearts Club Band laughing all the while – for although Tour player bonuses are as rare as hen's teeth, dividends from Prof's betting syndicate No.2 Fund in which we all have a 1/17th Man share are more reliable.

MARCH 26
Day 5 – Fourth Test – Delhi

Well, it should be Day 5, but it seems like an age since we got rolled and the tour was put out of its misery. There are a few sore heads around this morning, especially amongst the support staff, who really cut loose last night at the end of a tense five weeks. Darren made the terrible mistake of having a few more beers than he's used to, leaving his judgment somewhat impaired. He kept angling for information about the location of the "after-after party" – which is strictly "players only". It was Rabbit who stepped up to the plate, making his only contribution of the whole tour. He whispered something in Darren's ear, slipping him a piece of paper. Darren read it and nodded slowly. A few minutes later, he snuck out of the room, and hasn't been seen since.

We only got Rabbit to confess at lunch time. Instead of a complicated plan, he had gone done the simple route – told Darren to go to his room and wait for someone to ring him and let him know where the party was. "Oops, forgot to ring him!" said Rabbit, to raucous applause from the squad.

The members of the team who are about to play in the IPL are very nervous. There's talk in the media that those selected for The Ashes shouldn't be preparing for facing the skillful English swingers by playing hit and giggle on the flat India pitches. No-one wants to give up their IPL contract, but on the other hand, everyone wants to be thought of as so important for the Ashes Tour that they are asked to miss the IPL. Every phone call is answered as if it's from Cricket Australia, but so far, only the Captain and his dicky back will be sitting out.

Those of us who didn't get an IPL contract - we're not bitter at all – are packing up to return home tonight. I saw Wicky carrying three large black plastic bags down to the incinerator room himself, shrugging off all offers of help from hotel staff. He obviously didn't want the contents falling into souvenir hunters' hands. Or anyone else's.

It's hard to believe it's all over, and even harder to believe that I made it from being a rank outsider to actually making my Test Debut. I even scored a few under pressure, so maybe I've moved up a notch in the eyes of the Selectors – both the current ones and any others who might be appointed in their place. Not that I think that they should be replaced. Or that any new ones won't be as good. You get the idea.

Bring on The Ashes!

ABOUT THE AUTHORS

Dave Cornford

I was a stodgy but reliable opening bat in the lower grades. My SS Jumbo was too heavy to manoeuver towards the leg side, but my off-side driving was fearsome. Over my career I tried my hand at bowling everything that wasn't fast, with no real success. My greatest moment on field came at the end of a long year of floggings. We were chasing 88 in the second dig to win our only outright of the year. I opened and we were soon 2 for 10, our long suffering Captain despairing. With 33 no (my highest score) and a partnership of 80 for the third wicket, we brought it home for an 8 wicket triumph. I then moved to Sydney.

I now send a lot of time watching my teenage sons play junior cricket - one a fast bowling all-rounder with a straight bat and quick feet, the other an off-spinning all-rounder whose batting often results in the ball "staying hit."

The rest of the time I work as a consultant with a small tech start-up company, and write and self-publish fiction.

You can catch up on the rest of Dave's writing

At his blog: www.davecornford.com
On Twitter: @David_the_C
On Facebook

Jeremy Pooley

I've been in the corporate environment advising the great and the good for over 20 years about how to optimise the corporate machine, and as an entrepreneur. My LinkedIn profile is up to date, finally. I was a 'sometimes' cricketer, a much better cover fielder than left-arm seamer or right hand (sometimes good for 25) bat.

My worst defeat. Lost a game on a final ball run out because my partner held onto his box instead of diving into the crease.

My best victory. Coming from behind playing backyard cricket, 9 down, 1 to bowl, and 3 to get. Smashed a window for 6 on the last ball to win. Hid in the garage until it was safe to come out.

I like nothing better than to turn on the box, turn up the radio or tune in to ESPN, and relax for a few overs with whatever child is at hand, especially if rain has stopped play in the backyard.

KEEP IN TOUCH

You can hear more about The 17th Man, and keep up with blog posts, special offers and new releases, by subscribing at 17thmandiary.com.

Printed in Great Britain
by Amazon

34413700R00057